THE NOM WAH COOKBOOK

RECIPES AND STORIES FROM
100 YEARS AT NEW YORK CITY'S ICONIC
DIM SUM RESTAURANT

WILSON TANG
WITH JOSHUA DAVID STEIN

PHOTOGRAPHY BY ALEX LAU
ILLUSTRATIONS BY MARAL VAROLIAN

An Imprint of HarperCollins*Publishers*

CONTENTS

A NOTE ON ROMANIZATION VII
INTRODUCTION IX
THINGS YOU'LL NEED 1
THE BIG THREE TECHNIQUES 10

BAO 12
DUMPLINGS 30
ROLLS 82
CAKES 108
RICE 126
NOODLES 139
BALLS 157
CHEF'S SPECIALS 169
FEASTS 191
VEGETABLES 213
DESSERTS 221

ACKNOWLEDGMENTS 243
INDEX 245

A NOTE ON ROMANIZATION

We have generally chosen to provide Chinese words in today's jyutping system for romanizing the pronunciation of gwong dung waa, the Cantonese dialect of Hong Kong and Guangdong province. For simplicity, we have not included the tonal numbers that accompany the romanization of each word. For certain foods, we have opted for the path of least resistance, using the spelling that is more popular and recognizable than its jyutping counterpart, such as char siu bao vs. caa siu baau.

The one exception where we employ pinyin (Mandarin phonetics) would be for soup dumplings, where the Mandarin term (*xiao long bao*, as opposed to the Cantonese *siu lung baau*) is far more popular—it even has its own acronym: XLB!

Where appropriate, we have included the Traditional Chinese (as opposed to Simplified Chinese) characters, which are used in Taiwan, Hong Kong, and Macau. For the sake of consistency for people living in the United States, we have generally followed US usage in writing given name preceding surname.

INTRODUCTION

At the crook of Doyers Street in New York's Chinatown—a street so crimped and cramped with history it's like time's taken a hairpin curve—you'll find Nom Wah Tea Parlor. Sewn into the side street like a jewel in a hem, Nom Wah has provided a temporary home for the weary, the lonely, the fatigued, and the famished for the last hundred years. The sign, written in English with Chinese characters below, blinks like a homing beacon. Inside, a cup of scalding tea is always there for the sipping alongside an almond cookie or a steamer full of har gow for anyone who needs nourishment.

Push open the glass doors and the sound of porcelain knocking against porcelain still ricochets around the room. Even as the world outside has changed, the crack and cackle of teacup on table has been a steady score. Any business a century old has had its ups and downs, its crescendos and diminuendos. Nom Wah is no different. It survived; now it flourishes.

In the Nom Wah I remember growing up, this clatter was accompanied by the click-clack of ivory mahjong tiles and the exhale of a thousand cheap cigarettes. Add to that the plaintive creak of dim sum trolleys threading through the dining room, the hiss of steam from the kitchen line, and my uncle Wally, who always had a word—or at least a grunt—for everyone who walked through his door. It was the soundtrack of the Chinese experience in New York for much of the twentieth century. Or at least *my* Chinese American experience in New York for much of the twentieth century.

Uncle Wally, a hardworking man of strong opinions squeezed into a few words, didn't start the Tea Parlor. Wally arrived in New York in 1950, a sixteen-year-old immigrant fleeing Mao's Great Leap Forward. Like the vast majority of early Chinatown arrivals, Wally came from Toishan, in the southern rim of the Guangdong province in Southern China, and—again like the vast many of early Chinatown arrivals—he found employment in the restaurant industry. By then, Nom Wah was already thirty years old, an institution in the constant flux of Chinatown life, started by Ed and May Choy, a family from Guangzhou, the capital of Guangdong. The Choys were driven into the restaurant business by the Chinese Exclusion Act, a shameful blight on the history of America that not only unconstitutionally restricted Chinese immigration but, through visa restrictions, forced those immigrants who did arrive into low-skilled, low-pay labor like restaurant work and hand laundries. Take a look around and you'll see how long-tailed those laws are and how hard generations of Chinese immigrants worked to move beyond them.

Under the Choy family, the Tea Parlor was largely a bakery specializing in delicately flavored red bean–filled moon cakes, a specialty eaten in Guangdong in particular during the Chinese New Year, and, of course, tea. Dim sum, which is traditionally a breakfast food, was available in the early morning toward lunch. Before heading to work, folks would stop by for a few moments to grab a fried egg crepe stuffed with vegetables or a pillowy char siu bao, a steamed bun with bits of sweet roast pork inside.

Under the Choys, Wally worked his way up from dishwasher to cook to waiter to manager. Finally, when the couple retired in 1974, he bought the business—and 11–13 Doyers Street, the squat building that housed it. Continuing their tradition, he ran the place as a bakery but shifted his focus to include wholesale as well. After taking over the adjoining storefront, Nom Wah became known for its red bean paste and lotus seed paste, two essential components for Chinese bakeries.

Though the focus shifted, dim sum still wobbled on. It was easier to keep the restaurant going than to fold it up, so he still made sure there were snacks coming out of the kitchen. Making their rounds were carts laden with the classics: har gow, the pinkish shrimp visible through nearly translucent wrappers; golden squares of sausage-studded turnip cake; shimmering rice rolls called *cheung fun* topped with a sweet vinegary sauce and chunks of garlic-marinated spareribs.

I watched Nom Wah from afar. My father was also in the restaurant business until he retired a few years ago. When I was a kid, he had a takeout shop on the Upper West Side, and he also ran a wholesale company selling Chinese products to Chinese restaurants. Later he founded a travel agency. But when I was a kid we moved from the cramped confines of Chinatown into the outer boroughs. Some families ended up in Ridgewood or Flushing. We ended up in Middle Village, Queens. On the weekends, he always brought me back to Nom Wah, back to Chinatown, back to the traditions and a taste of home.

I was born in 1978, so I remember Nom Wah best starting in the 1980s and 1990s. By then the place was in a state of decline. Increasing free trade with China had introduced to the market Chinese-made red bean and lotus seed paste that was better and, though it was shipped from Guangzhou, cheaper than what Wally could make. What's more, Chinatown itself was emptying out of Toisanese immigrants,

many of whom, like my dad, had climbed up the socioeconomic ladder and bought houses outside of Manhattan. They were replaced, increasingly, by Fujianese immigrants, who not only spoke a different dialect but had their own distinct culture, culinary traditions, and family associations. Nom Wah soldiered on as an informal social club for the OG dim sum chefs in the neighborhood. After they got off the line from their 7 a.m. to 3 p.m. shift, they'd gather at my uncle's shop to shoot the shit for a few hours before they went home. Uncle Wally always had *something* to offer them, usually a tea and a cookie and a cigarette, but if they wanted something more than that, he'd head over to a nearby restaurant and order it for them. That is, if he liked you. It wasn't, to say the least, a customer-friendly experience, but Wally didn't seem to care. "I own the building," he'd say, "I can do what I want with it."

Although he never outright shuttered the restaurant, Nom Wah was carried through the late '90s and the early aughts by salutary neglect. Wally was right. He owned the building outright and could do with it what he wanted. Mostly he didn't want to do anything, just let the Nom Wah he had grown old in remain untouched. The floor stayed worn, the walls etched and cracked by time, the tabletops grooved from decades of elbows. One unexpected outgrowth of this was that Nom Wah became popular as a film

set. It was a frequent backdrop for *Law & Order*. Uncle Wally loved it because he didn't have to do anything to make $5,000 a day, and the film crews loved it because Wally let them do whatever they wanted.

As Nom Wah's fortunes declined, mine were on the rise. I had always studied hard and done well at school. In 2000, after graduating from Pace University, I got a job as a financial analyst for Morgan Stanley. I had never seen my parents so proud. In many ways, my entrance into the white-collar professions validated— and vindicated—the years of sacrifice they had made. It's hard to imagine—but so common—that a mere two generations ago, the Tangs had been impoverished immigrants with little purchase in the country. Now I was a cog in the new fevered economy. Not just a cog either. I was a driver. But I made for an unhappy chauffeur.

True, I had a knack for and interest in business, but being rooted to an office chair staring at a computer screen for hours felt like some sort of slow-burn death, a surrender at such a tender age. I knew this was what my parents had worked so hard for, yet it was profoundly not what I wanted. I think they sensed it too.

I had always kept my eye on Nom Wah, and as I felt the tendrils of the corporate world cinch tighter and tighter around my neck, I yearned to return to it. I knew it was precious, a diamond in the rough—

but one that was in danger of blinking out completely. Wally was old. The space was older still and the clientele sat around mostly because they couldn't stand up anymore.

September 11, 2001, had dealt a near-fatal blow to Chinatown, closing the district to business and customers. Many small businesses, factories, and restaurants didn't make it through. Nom Wah did, but just barely. It took a lot out of Wally, and by 2010, he was ready to hang up his hat. What would become of Nom Wah? Both he and my dad knew I had an interest in the business. And so one day they took me to a modern dim sum restaurant with bare white walls and Chinese lanterns—plus a few disco balls hanging from the ceiling—in SoHo, a few blocks from Nom Wah.

"Wilson," said Wally, "how would you feel about taking over the business?"

"Take a look around," my dad continued. "You could turn it into something like this! Do with it what you want!"

I was flattered. I was terrified, but I was ready. But I knew, though, that what I wanted to do with Nom Wah was keep it just as it was—preserved in time as a jewel of Chinatown past, a monument to the generations before me—and at the same time prepare it for a hundred years in the future.

Thus began an adventure that would come to consume me and that would bring me ever closer to both my Chinatown roots and my identity as an American.

WHEN I TOOK OVER NOM WAH IN 2010, I didn't do much on the surface, save for a modest facelift. The old counter circa the 1930s remains; the black-and-white tile floor is still there and the teacups are mismatched. What I focused on restoring was what came out of the kitchen. I wanted to elevate the traditional dim sum we served to the highest standards. During a months-long renovation, I replaced the half-century-old kitchen equipment with a state-of-the-art line. When we reopened, I abolished the traditional dim sum carts in which dumplings and bao would sit for hours. Instead, we instituted a cooked-to-order system—accompanied by the now-familiar ordering sheet—that ensured we'd be serving the freshest ingredients to our guests. Gradually and to the fury of traditionalists, I changed the closing time from 3 p.m. to 10 p.m., extending dim sum from a morning meal through dinner and turning it into a late-night snack as well.

Most of the work was unseen. With the help of Chef Wun Gaw Kong, who had worked with Wally in the 1980s before turning dim sum journeyman, we broke down each element of the menu at Nom Wah and rebuilt it from scratch with an eye toward quality. Dim sum isn't about reinventing the wheel. It grows from a culinary tradition that stretches back to the first century BC, when roadside teahouses dotted the Silk Road as it snaked through

Southern China. Travelers, merchants, and migrants would rest their bones and warm themselves with bottomless cups of tea and small steamed snacks to aid in digestion. The dumplings, the turnip pancakes, the wide flat rice noodles that we serve at Nom Wah in 2018 are close cousins, siblings perhaps, sons or daughters even, of what my ancestors ate thousands of years ago. Like I said, we're not reinventing the wheel. We're just trueing the spokes.

But, as I've seen many of the businesses I grew up with in Chinatown peter out of

existence, I'm equally aware that for Nom Wah to move into the future, I can't allow a historical gaze to prevent me from looking forward. Using all that I learned in my stints in business school and in finance, I've extended dim sum beyond the four walls of Nom Wah Tea Parlor with outposts in Philadelphia and more contemporary outposts in the downtown Manhattan neighborhoods of Nolita and the Lower East Side. There are even Nom Wahs scattered throughout China. I've pushed for collaborations that Wally could never contemplate, making a chopped cheese dumpling with Adidas and an "everything" bao with my friends at Katz's Delicatessen and Russ & Daughters. I've brought on non-Chinese partners including Julie Cole, a brilliant young NYU grad who now heads the kitchen at Nom Wah Nolita. Julie's brought her own thirst for innovation and the chops to fit the entire world into a dim sum wrapper. With every innovation, I've had to face the resistance of dim sum traditionalists—very few of them Chinese. But I tell them dim sum is a living tradition. It isn't a museum piece, and neither is Nom Wah.

This book is more than a cookbook. It captures the voices of my Chinatown community, of the artisans and tradespeople who carry on the culinary traditions of the last millennia. It's a story of adapting some traditions *for* the future while safeguarding some *from* the future. Though it is my journey as a restaurateur, it isn't just my story.

Here you'll find the recipes my family has been perfecting for generations, the recipes that have nourished visitors to Nom Wah for nearly a century. You'll learn how to make our delicate dumpling wrappers—and where to buy them if you don't have the time—then how to fold them into neat packages and fill them with an array of iterative fillings: shrimp, shrimp and pork, pork and chive, and more. You'll also find the secrets to our best-selling "original" egg roll and the technique behind our toothsome char siu, which can be served either on its own or secreted into the center of a lily-white bun. Pan-fried noodles, all things rice, a treasury of steamed treats, the almond cookie and the moon cake, the lotus cake and the phoenix bun: they're all here. But you'll also find dim sum reaching out into the world, embracing modern trends.

More important—perhaps most important to me—you'll hear from a chorus of voices that make Nom Wah Nom Wah, the chorus that makes Chinatown as vibrant today as it was back in 1920, when Nom Wah first opened. Each of these stories—many of them stories I heard for the first time through the process of writing this book—mirrors mine in some way and

also differs in the small and large ways that make each of us unique. If you're Chinese or Chinese American, chances are you've heard some version of this story from your grandparents or parents. (Although, let's face it: Chinese immigrants of certain age have a remarkable ability to answer the most profound questions with the most cursory grunts or just straight-up silence.) Perhaps these stories have been amalgamated into demographics and statistics you've ingested, but the reason we've included these stories, which, like dim sum itself, are largely theme and variation, is because when read together, they convey something essential to the nature of Chinatown and thus to the nature of Nom Wah.

Of course, things have changed. Walk into the Tea Parlor today and you're just as likely to hear English, Italian, French, and Spanish alongside the Cantonese and Mandarin. Mahjong tiles have been replaced by smartphones. Cigarette smoke, of course, is long gone. By remaining true to our roots but allowing change to blossom naturally, we've become a tourist destination as well as a local favorite. But underneath the languages and bustle, you'll still hear the clatter of porcelain on porcelain, cup on saucer, and saucer on table. It's the heartbeat of Nom Wah, a hundred years strong.

THE NOM WAH COOKBOOK

THINGS YOU'LL NEED

HARDWARE

Dim sum is meant to be both easy to make and easy to eat. There's not a ton of kitchen stuff you'll need for any of these recipes—no immersion circulator or specialized gadget that cubes a melon and flays a fish in a single swipe. But it is a non-Western cooking vernacular, and there are a few things that will make your overall experience a zillion times easier. The good news is—Chinese people in general and dim sum cooks in particular being flinty and resourceful—these few tools can be used for nearly everything. I've seen kitchens where they are nearly the *only* utensils. Those are often the best kitchens.

A WOK: Featured in the majority of bad puns in strip mall Chinese joints, the wok is also one of China's greatest culinary exports. First used by the Mongols two thousand years ago, the wok is a large circular pan—*wok* is Cantonese for "cooking pot" or "pan"— that gets super hot super fast. The best woks are thin and made of cast-iron or steel. Traditionally, they've got a round bottom, but a flat bottom is good too, especially for American stoves. (Chinese stoves often have an opening in which the wok sits, bringing it even closer to the flame.)

In terms of size, I mean woks can get crazy big. The woks we use at Nom Wah are 32 inches in diameter. But don't worry, I'm not tryna monopolize your kitchen space. For at-home use, a 12-inch or a 16-inch wok will be just fine. The wok should be big enough for you to toss whatever is inside it around without the ingredients going over the edge like some bad-luck kid in a poorly designed waterslide.

THINGS YOU CAN DO WITH A WOK:

You can steam in it (see page 10).
You can stir-fry in it (see page 11).
You can stew in it.
You can boil in it.
You can use it as a big bowl.

A WOK LID: This is especially useful for steaming, obviously. Get an aluminum one with a little wooden knob on top.

A WOK RING: If you're going to use the traditional round-bottomed wok, you'll also need a wok ring or wok stand. It is exactly what it sounds like and sits on your stovetop.

A WOK CHUAN: Due to the curved nature of the wok, a traditional flat spatula is an awkward fit. The harmonious curves of a wok chuan—or wok spatula—nestle in cutely to the curves. There's also such a thing as a wok spoon, but a wok spatula is sufficiently shovel-like to do double duty.

A SPIDER: As you'll see in the following pages, dim sum is mostly about submerging dim sum things in a hot liquid (oil or water) or shrouding them in hot vapors (steam). A spider, a long-handled mesh spoon with which you can remove dim sum things from water or steam, will be your friend here.

A STEAMER: There are many ways to improvise a steamer, but why go MacGyver when a good stainless steel, or bamboo, steamer basket is about $7 and fits in most pots, including a wok? But if you don't want to buy one, we'll teach you how to improvise on page 10.

A COTTON KITCHEN TOWEL: Many woks have long bamboo or metal handles. Traditional woks from Canton, however, have two looped handles on either side. They get crazy hot. Unless you're an OG like Wun Gaw who just grabs them like a maniac, you'll want to protect yourself with a folded-up kitchen towel.

A CHINESE CLEAVER: In the hands of a dim sum chef, a Chinese cleaver is a thing of beauty. It can be used for everything from hacking apart a full-on suckling pig to chopping gai lan (Chinese broccoli). What you're looking for is a stainless-steel blade with some weight in it. Most traditional cleavers are rectangular with a heavy heel, though new cleavers tend to be slightly lighter with an angled spine. Whichever you choose, keep your knife like you keep yourself: looking sharp.

THINGS YOU CAN DO WITH A CLEAVER:

You can chop through bone.

You can slice with it.

You can use the side of it to smash stuff.

You can use it as a shovel.

You can use it as a teaspoon.

Or a tablespoon.

Or two.

PANTRY

Look, no one has unlimited kitchen space, not at the restaurant, not at home, and certainly not in Chinatown, where the apartments are the size of air bubbles. Yet to properly cook dim sum there are a few key pantry ingredients you'd do well to purchase. For the most part, they last a long time and, in the Chinese way, do double, sometimes triple, duty. Yeah, you can get all of them from Amazon and have them delivered to your door within twenty-four hours, but I'd suggest finding your local Asian grocery store and going there. You'll meet new people. You'll see new things. C'mon, it's good for you to be out and about.

DARK SOY SAUCE: Get yourself a bottle of lou cau, or dark soy sauce. Less salty than its lighter cousin, we use this mostly to add color to dishes like egg fried rice and pork belly casserole. Our preferred brand is Pearl River Bridge Superior Dark Soy Sauce.

LIGHT SOY SAUCE: This is your workhorse soy sauce, endower of salty flavor, marinator of meats, serenader of vegetables. It's what olive oil is to Italian food or butter is to the French. "Light" here indicates color, not level of sodium or anything. (In fact, light soy sauce is saltier than dark.) Kikkoman brand is just fine, though be aware that since Kikkoman is known for their light soy sauce, the label won't say "light." It'll just say soy sauce.

TOASTED SESAME OIL: One of the earliest known crop oils, toasted sesame oil has a wonderfully nutty flavor and hardly ever turns rancid. We use Kadoya toasted sesame oil, the gold standard.

CHICKEN POWDER: A descendent of chicken bouillon—which can also be used in a pinch—chicken powder is a flavor-rich powdered stock. We use Hong Kong's Lee Kum Kee chicken powder, the OG stuff, though Knorr works well too.

FERMENTED BLACK BEANS: Odiferous and complex fermented black beans, called *dau*

3

si, have been made in China since 200 BC. They are too intense to eat alone yet are wonderfully umami-rich companions to meats like spareribs and chicken feet. Get the kind in the cool yellow container with ginger called Yang Jiang.

MSG: Yeah, you'll see a lot of MSG in these recipes. Why? Mostly because we got tired of writing out monosodium glutamate. Are you concerned? Don't be. It's true, MSG was an invented thing. It was invented by a Japanese food scientist named Kikunae Ikeda in 1908 as a sort of distillate of kombu, the umami-rich kelp we call *haidai* in Chinese. But you know what else is also invented? Air-conditioning. Also cars, Honeycrisp apples, and Diet Coke. That doesn't stop anyone, does it?

Basically, MSG is a flavor enhancer. It's like a bright yellow highlighter for your taste buds. It's in nearly every American snack food from Doritos to Chick-fil-A sandwiches. As an owner of a dim sum restaurant, I've had to hear about "Chinese restaurant syndrome," the dubious claim that MSG causes headaches and other symptoms, for years. But there's been no scientific evidence to establish a connection, except, I guess, outdated and offensive tropes about cheap Chinese food.

That being said, in none of these recipes is MSG a necessary ingredient. Your favorite book is still your favorite book even without the highlighting. The prose is just as tasty, though your favorite lines might be harder to find.

OYSTER SAUCE: A condiment made not for oysters but out of them, oyster sauce was invented by accident—like penicillin!—in 1888 by Lee Kum Sheung, founder of Lee Kum Kee, after he overcooked the oysters at his Hong Kong oyster stall. The dark sauce makes every noodle, every rice roll, better.

SHAOXING WINE: Often called Chinese cooking wine, Shaoxing is made with fermented rice and tastes a little like a dry sherry. As with all cooking wines, get yourself something you'd drink straight. I like Pagoda Huadiao brand—just make sure you get the kind without salt.

RICE WINE VINEGAR: Less acidic than Western white vinegar, rice wine vinegar (also called simply rice vinegar) is delicately flavored and slightly sweet. Along with soy sauce and toasted sesame oil, it makes up the flavorful underpainting of many dishes.

AJI-MIRIN: Like Shaoxing, aji-mirin is a cooking wine made with rice. Unlike Shaoxing, it's sweeter and a bit more complex and actually hails from Japan. Kikkoman has a pretty good and widely available aji-mirin, under the name Kikkoman Manjo Aji-Mirin.

RICE: There are two types of rice: glutinous (or sticky) and regular. Buy a pound of each. We use sticky rice for sticky rice and Chinese sausage; we use regular rice for fried rice and as an accompaniment to most of the big format dishes.

RICE FLOUR: Just as there are two types of rice: regular and glutinous, there are two types of rice flour: regular and glutinous. We use regular rice flour as a base for many of our steamed rice dishes from turnip cakes to rice rolls. (Glutinous rice flour, which turns chewy when fried, is used often for thickening sauces and in desserts but isn't used as frequently.) The flours look identical, which can be confusing. We use Erawan brand from Thailand. The regular rice flour has the red label.

CORNSTARCH: Though flavorless itself, cornstarch is an integral ingredient to mastering the stir-fry. Not only does it seal the flavors into the food being fried, but it adds body to the sauce and ensures an even coating.

POTATO STARCH: Unlike cornstarch, potato starch is a root starch. Though one can be substituted for the other in a

pinch, we prefer potato starch for frying and cornstarch for thickening due to their varying properties over high heat.

DRIED SHRIMP: These small, salted, and sun-dried shrimps are the Allen Iversons of dim sum. They're nibblet-sized umami bombs that have a disproportional impact on your quality of life. Make sure you get dried shrimp that are bright orange, not faded peach.

DRIED SHIITAKE MUSHROOMS: Along with dried shrimp, dried shiitake mushrooms are the secret weapon in the dim sum kitchen. Similarly rich with umami, the mushrooms—also called dried black mushrooms—find their way into soups, fillings, rice dishes, anything that would benefit from some texture, body, and backbone. Much easier to find and

obviously with a longer shelf life than fresh shiitake mushrooms, these must be hydrated before use. To do that, just soak the things in warm water for 15 to 20 minutes, until the mushrooms are tender. Remove, pat dry, and they're ready to use.

CHINESE SAUSAGE (LAP CHEONG): Lap cheong refers to all sausage from China, so it's a little like saying you should have charcuterie in your pantry if you're going to cook Italian. But the type of Chinese sausage most often used in Cantonese cooking is a very dry, very sweet variety that also happens to be called lap cheong. It's an air-cured sausage made with pork and seasoned with, among other things, liquor. The type of liquor—whether it is rice wine, rose wine, or sorghum liquor—determines the sweetness and character of the sausage. You'll find packages of the stuff in most Asian groceries. We get ours from Sun Ming Jan on Hester Street. It makes cameos in the sticky rice with Chinese sausage (page 131) and the turnip cake (page 114), but I also sometimes just dice it up and fold it into eggs when I make omelets for my kids.

SAMBAL OELEK: True, sambal oelek hails from Indonesia, not China, but we're huge fans of this spicy-as-hell paste made with ground fresh chili peppers and vinegar. Some sambal oelek contains additional flavors, but we prefer Huy Fong's, which has nothing but vinegar, peppers, and salt.

PICKLED RED CHILI: Another endower of heat and spice comes from Guizhou, in south-central China, a province that combines the heat-seeking Szechuan style with a love of all things sour. This is best embodied in these pickled red chilis. We use the Cock on the Mountain Top Brand, often shortened to the Cock Brand, which makes me laugh every time.

CHILI OIL: The final spice agent from Guizhou is chili oil, a mixture of star anise, cinnamon, bay leaves, chili flakes, Szechuan peppercorns, and a bunch of other spices suspended in oil. We use Lao Gan Ma's Spicy Chili Crisp or Dynasty Hot Chili Oil. You should put this on everything.

FRIED GARLIC: Though relatively easy to make yourself, keep a jar of fried garlic on hand in those cases when just a sprinkle is needed as a garnish. It's available at most Asian grocery stores. We use the Aroy-D brand, but Maesri is a good alternative.

HOW THIS WHOLE BOOK WORKS

Like I said, dim sum isn't about setting aside hours of your day to listen to NPR podcasts and leisurely prepare elaborate feasts with a hundred components, a thousand techniques, dots and dashes of sauce, and other sorts of edible frippery. Not that there's anything wrong with that, but that's not what this is.

Dim sum is a system devised to create maximum deliciousness with minimum effort. It is made and eaten by people for whom time is a precious resource. To that end, since time immemorial dim sum kitchens have optimized their menus, building mansions out of just a few basic building blocks wisely, and repeatedly, used. Dim sum is more like a Harold Pinter play featuring a few well-developed characters than a Vegas revue. Dim sum is like SEAL Team Six rather than an infantry platoon, agile but not gargantuan. Dim sum is like Philip Glass, not Arnold Schoenberg: a limited vocabulary of notes, cannily repeated. It's more Mondrian than Bonnard. It's like the Royal Air Force in the Battle of Britain: never has so much relied on so few. There are more similes in this paragraph than there are components in traditional dim sum.

How to capture that in a book has, frankly, been a challenge. The whole premise of cookbooks is to fill their pages with enough words and techniques and photographs and whatever else so when you get home, you don't feel cheated. Hopefully you won't, but ¯_(ツ)_/¯ .

Cheating is what the dim sum kitchen does. We cheat time. We cheat energy. I'm perfectly happy admitting that Nom Wah, like every other dim sum parlor on Earth, is a shell game. We create feasts that feed thousands of people—feasts that feed families of people—with an astonishingly short ingredient list.

So that's the secret and that's the way this book works. I figured the most useful way to share these recipes would be to lay out the organizational system of the kitchen—that is, the epistemological scaffolding—up front. This is the Grand Theory of Dim Sum, and it will be your guide for the rest of the book.

FILLINGS VERSUS WRAPPERS

Dim sum can be divided into two. There are the wrappers and there are the fillings. Of wrappers, we're talking everything from silken bean curd to translucent crystal skin, gelatinous and milky rice rolls, yeasty bao, and more. Of fillings, well anything that isn't a wrapper can be a filling. (Also, sometimes, the wrapper is the filling.) Primus inter pares are the three Master Fillings we use over and over again. They are the Pork Master Filling, the Shrimp Master Filling, and the No Pork No Shrimp Master Filling. You'll find these recipes at the beginning of the Dumplings chapter (page 30) because that's where their story begins. Unlike other, more versatile fillings like steamed spareribs, which can be eaten sheathed or not, these Master Fillings feel exposed when un-dumplinged. They are like hermit crabs without their shells. But they are reliable, versatile, and trustworthy

CLOCKWISE FROM TOP-LEFT: Har Gow (p. 69); Pork Siu Mai (p. 65); House Special Pan-Fried Pork Dumplings (p. 45); Shrimp and Snow Pea Leaf Har Gow (p. 69); Shrimp and Chive Har Gow (p. 69)

companions, the kinds of fillings you can take to a cocktail party or an art opening and they'll mingle just fine.

Similar to fillings, some wrappers are codependent and some have a healthy sense of self. Bao, for instance, can either be empty bao or filled bao. Rice rolls can either be plain or stuffed. But a dumpling without a dumpling filling isn't a something. It's a nothing. Tofu skin without its innards is a tragedy. At their best, wrappers are containers, methods of conveyance, and carby foils to their protein cargo. They are the id to the fillings' ego and should never be taken for granted.

« MIDDLE: House Special Pan-Fried Pork Dumplings (p. 45)
BOTTOM: Sweet Potato Kale Wontons (p. 54)

THE BIG THREE TECHNIQUES

As an outgrowth of its origins as roadside teahouse fare, most traditional dim sum dishes are steamed. A good number these days are also pan-fried or stir-fried (the deep fryer didn't really enter the dim sum kitchen until the twentieth century). Much of the action happens in the wok, which, as noted, is a versatile tool.

In terms of techniques we use, there are two that loom large. We steam. We pan-fry. (We also deep-fry, bake, and roast, but much more rarely.) Instead of writing these instructions over and over again, I'm putting the basic techniques here. The method below presupposes you have a wok, a skillet, and a steamer, which, if you followed our advice, you'll have already purchased. However, the logic of the techniques holds true even with a large lidded pot to replace the wok and a sheet pan to replace the steamer.

HOW TO STEAM

Steaming is perhaps what sets dim sum apart from all other dumpling-loving kitchens of the world. We steam everything at Nom Wah in an industrial Vulcan steamer. At home, I recommend steaming in a wok. Steaming times vary depending on the density and size of what you are steaming. But the general

setup to steam in a wok is as follows.

Fill the wok with enough water to come up to the lower rim of the steamer but not so much the waterline is above the food bed. Line the bottom of the steamer with paper or a lotus leaf or something so that the fiddly bits won't fall through the cracks. (If steaming dumplings or bao, you won't need to line the steamer.) Place whatever needs steaming in the basket, leaving ample room between items. Bring water to boil and steam for the desired duration. If you need more water—water tends to evaporate—add boiling, not cold, water so as not to stop the steaming.

If you *do* want to DIY it, just use a plate in a pot. All you need is tinfoil and a plate that fits in your pot. Fill a pot with ½ an inch of water. Then make a sort of tripod out of tinfoil by forming three golf ball–sized balls and placing them in the bottom of the pot,

making sure their tops rest above the water-line. Rest the plate on the tinfoil, cover, and steam. This method is especially useful when making rice rolls, in which you'll be using a cake pan instead of the plate.

You can put anything in the steamer as long as it isn't so small that it would tumble through the holes into the roiling waters below.

HOW TO PAN-FRY

For most ingredients that are pan-fried, it's best to use a nonstick pan. In the case of dumplings, we pan-fry *after* we steam, in order to imbue them with that pleasingly crunchy, slightly sweet wrapper. To prepare, heat neutral oil over medium-high heat in a large nonstick pan until shimmering. Place

steamed dumplings, fold to the side, in the pan starting from the center outward. Turn after a minute, let brown for another minute, then remove to a paper towel–lined plate when golden brown.

HOW TO STIR-FRY IN A WOK

There's a reason that stir-frying in the wok is the ultimate station in traditional Cantonese kitchens. Woks get so blazingly hot that the difference between burned to hell and pleasingly crispy is a few milliseconds. But the wok's superpower of heat transference is also the source of wok hei, the famous Cantonese "breath of wok," the alchemical reactions that occur between spice and noodles, protein or whatever else you've got in there at such astronomical temperatures.

The key to stir-frying in a wok is constant agitation and alacrity. Watching Wun Gaw at the wok is like standing in the pit of an F1 race. The ingredients go in with one hand while the other, hand grasping the handle, is already tossing the ingredients in graceful loops. We use stir-fry technique especially in the later chapters. It should be done in a manner of minutes. Just remember to agitate constantly.

As for the wrappers, the recipes for those and their techniques for folding or rolling are found in their relevant chapter; dumplings for dumplings, bao for bao, and rolls and rice for those too.

BAO

CLOCKWISE FROM TOP: Vegetable Bao (p. 22); House
Special Roast Pork Buns (p. 20); Mantao (p. 19)

Back in the early days of dim sum, there were no ovens along the Silk Road, so everything, bread included, was steamed—a far simpler process than baking. One of the best things that emerged from the clouds of steam was the bao, pillowy rolls of moist lily-white dough filled with morsels of protein.

You could write an entire cookbook—hell, fill a library even—with recipes for bao. Bao just means a stuffed bun, and a stuffed bun can be as great and varied as whatever is in it. In the world of dim sum, and more generally grab-and-go Chinese food (which is most Chinese food), bao holds a place of privilege. It is the grabbiest-and-go-iest (and gooiest and goodest) street snack. You don't need chopsticks. You don't need a plate. You just need hands and a mouth.

As a kid, I cheerfully joined in the Bao Army. Rushing from Kaplan tutoring to Chinese school on Saturday mornings, I used to grab a steaming bun for 50 cents at the no-frills Mei Li Wah Bakery and eat it while rushing after my mom who refused to slow down for me. Now I do the same thing to my kids. Bao feeds everyone from students rushing to get to school to day laborers with but a few minutes to fuel themselves before hours of work. It is a staple of the Chinatown bakeries and coffeehouses that serve as meeting spots and third places for senior citizens with limited income but hella free time. Walk into Tai Pan Bakery on Canal Street, one of my favorites, and you'll see sweet and savory bao, from yellow-topped pineapple buns (bo lo bao) to red bean buns to mantao, the most basic of all buns: empty steamed buns.

Unlike most dim sum, bao originally comes from Northern China, where the main carbs were wheat and millet, as opposed to rice in the South. Culinary historians pinpoint the birth of mantao to the Three Kingdoms period in the third century AD. It's a crazy story. I hope to God it's true. The word is that this chancellor, Zhuge Liang, was returning home to the North after subduing a bunch of Southern "barbarians." These barbarians had the nasty habit of using human heads as sacrifice. So when my man Zhuge couldn't get his victorious troops across the Lu River—the river being turbid and dangerous—these Southern "barbarians," now conquered, suggested he behead some of his troops, toss their domes into the water to appease the river gods, and ford the river. Zhuge demurred. But what he did do was have his men wrap some chopped-up beef and lamb in dough, sculpt the dough to look like heads, and throw *those* into the river to trick the gods. It worked. He called the buns "barbarians heads," or in Cantonese, *mantao*. I'll let the *gweilo* have their Earl of Sandwich with his one-handed gambling addiction. I'll take Zhuge Liang and his barbarian heads any day of the week.

BASIC BAO DOUGH

MAKES 10 BUNS

What makes our buns so good is that we use a mix of yeast and baking powder as leavening agents in the dough. Many restaurants rely solely on the baking powder for leavening, but that leads to a bitter and stickier dough. Adding yeast to the mixture, however, gives the bun fluffiness.

1 teaspoon active dry yeast
1½ cups warm water
3 cups all-purpose flour
6 tablespoons sugar
2 tablespoons neutral oil
1½ teaspoons baking powder

IN the bowl of an electric mixer fitted with the dough hook attachment, sift the flour and sugar. Add the yeast and baking powder. **ADD** the water and oil slowly while mixing on the lowest speed until a smooth dough ball forms, 1 to 2 minutes. (You can do this by hand, as well, though it will take longer.) **COVER** the dough with a damp cloth and let rest for approximately 2 hours, until it doubles in size. (This is a perfect time, by the way, to make your fillings for the bao.) **TURN** the dough out onto a flat surface and gently knead by hand until the dough becomes smooth again, approximately 5 minutes. If the dough is dry, add 1 to 2 teaspoons of water. Cover with a damp cloth and let rest for another 15 minutes.

WHILE the dough rests, lay out ten flattened cupcake liners (alternatively, you can cut a large piece of parchment paper into ten 4 x 4-inch squares). These are your bao coasters.

TO make the buns, roll the dough into a tube approximately 2 inches in diameter and 1½ to 2 feet long and divide it into 10 equal pieces.

REROLL each piece of dough into a disc about 4½ inches in diameter and about ¼ inch thick. They should be thicker in the center and thinner around the edges.

ADD about 2 tablespoons filling to the center of the dough and pleat the buns until they're closed on top.

SET up a steamer according to the instructions on page 10. Place each bun on a cupcake liner (or parchment paper square) and steam for 12 minutes until bun is firm to touch with a little bit of give. Serve immediately.

HOW TO STUFF AND CLOSE A BAO

STEP 1. Hold the disc of dough in one hand.

STEP 2. Scoop 2 tablespoons of filling into the center.

STEP 3. Close the bao slightly by cupping your hand gently.

STEP 4. Using your thumb and pointer finger of the opposite hand, gather a bit of dough to form a ¼-inch-deep pleat. Press firmly to seal. Use your middle finger to gather the next pleat, then transfer that pleat to join the previous pleat between the thumb and pointer, pressing together again. Advance your fingers around the edge, gathering, pinching, and pressing, 12 to 14 pleats. As you go, use the thumb of the bao-holding hand to tuck the filling down slightly.

STEP 5. Once all the pleats have been gathered, twist the pleats together to help seal the bao and make it look pretty.

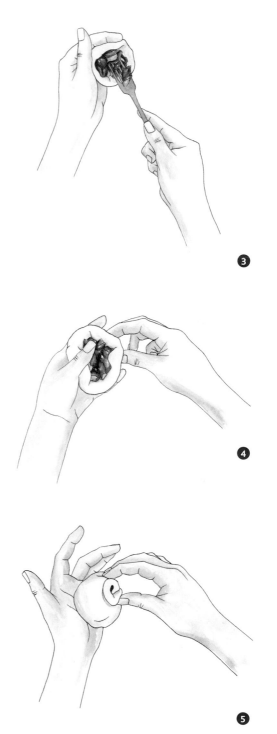

17

MANTAO

MAKES 15 BUNS

Mantao are the most basic of all bao. They are inchoate bao, potential bao, primordial and future bao. But they're also delicious in their own right. The keys to said deliciousness are twofold: First, add a little milk before you knead the dough, and second, make the mantao smaller than stuffed bao. Each should be about 2 inches in diameter. Mantao always reminds me of a hole-less Chinese bagel, even more so when we sprinkle Everything Bagel seasoning on top of it, as pictured.

1 teaspoon active dry yeast
¾ cup warm water
3 cups all-purpose flour
5 tablespoons sugar
¼ cup neutral oil
¼ cup whole milk
2½ teaspoons baking powder
1 tablespoon of Everything Bagel seasoning
(optional—Trader Joe's makes a great
one; alternatively, use 1 teaspoon toasted
sesame seeds, 1 teaspoon poppy seeds,
1 teaspoon fried garlic, and 1 teaspoon salt)

IN the bowl of an electric mixer fitted with the dough hook attachment, dissolve the yeast in the warm water.

SIFT the flour and sugar into a separate large bowl. Add to the yeast mixture, then add the neutral oil and milk.

MIX on the lowest speed until a smooth dough ball forms, 1 to 2 minutes. (You can do this by hand, as well, though it will take longer.)

COVER the dough with a damp cloth and let rest for approximately 2 hours, until it doubles in size. Once rested, roll the dough out on a well-floured surface to a tube about ¼ inch thick and 18 to 24 inches long.

STARTING with the edge nearest you, roll the dough up into a cylinder, like you were forming a Cinnabon. Slice the roll lengthwise every ½ inch into 15 pieces. If you'd like to jazz up your bao, sprinkle each bun with the Everything Bagel seasoning, and press seasoning gently into dough.

SET up a steamer according to the instructions on page 10, add the mantao, and steam for 8 to 9 minutes until bun is firm to touch with a little bit of give. Serve immediately.

HOUSE SPECIAL ROAST PORK BUNS (CHAR SIU BAO)

MAKES 10 BUNS

As for the filling, this is just one way to use the ever-versatile char siu, which you'll also find in the Char Siu Family Meal (page 183) and Char Siu Noodles (page 143). In fact, BBQ pork bao is a great way to use up leftovers after a feast. But feel free to experiment with what you put in the bao—I've made it with glass noodles (carb on carb!) or leftover ground beef at home—but be aware that a too-liquidy filling will render your bao soggy, and no one wants a soggy bun.

1 tablespoon neutral oil
⅔ cup finely chopped white onion
2 tablespoons sugar
2 tablespoons light soy sauce
3 tablespoons oyster sauce
4 teaspoons toasted sesame oil
4 teaspoons dark soy sauce
3 cups chopped char siu (page 183)
1 teaspoon cornstarch
2 tablespoons water
1 recipe basic bao dough (page 16)

HEAT the neutral oil in a wok over medium-high heat until sizzling. Add the onion and stir-fry for 1 minute or until onions become translucent. In a separate small bowl, whisk together the sugar, light soy sauce, oyster sauce, toasted sesame oil, and dark soy sauce until fully combined. Turn the heat down on your wok to medium-low and add the char siu and sauce mixture. Cook, stirring on medium low heat until the mixture starts to bubble up and the sugar dissolves, approximately 5 minutes.

IN a separate bowl, combine the cornstarch and water to create a slurry—this will act as a thickener.

WHILE still bubbling, add in the slurry and stir immediately so that it is well incorporated. Stirring constantly, bring back to a boil/bubble then remove from heat.

SET aside to cool (If you make the filling ahead of time, cover and refrigerate to prevent it from drying out).

FILL the bao according to the instructions on page 17. Set up a steamer according to the instructions on page 10, add the bao, and steam for 12 to 15 minutes until bun is firm to touch with a little bit of give. Serve immediately.

VEGETABLE BAO

MAKES 10 BUNS

The traditional Cantonese diet was extremely veggie forward. Meat was expensive and most people were poor, so . . . there you have it. In the United States, however, for a variety of weird and sordid reasons, meat is often cheaper than vegetables—so dim sum tends to be heavy on the meat. Especially for first-gen Chinese immigrants, the ability to eat meat at nearly every meal was an indicator that they had finally made it. So this vegetable bao came not from Wun Gaw at Nom Wah OG but from Julie Cole at our more contemporary offshoot, Nom Wah Nolita. Pretty early on we realized that if we were going to have a sustainable lunch business, we needed to offer some veg options. It was funny to return to the Cantonese eating habits of a hundred years ago to find inspiration for modern fast casual, but time is a circle, blah blah blah, and you can't argue with the pure living satisfaction of sautéed gai lan with crunchy bits of bamboo shoot.

NOTE: *You'll need to make the filling the night before you make your bao.*

½ teaspoon kosher salt, plus more for blanching
2 pounds Chinese broccoli (gai lan)
2 tablespoons neutral oil
½ cup canned bamboo shoots, minced
½ cup minced dried bean curd (also called tofu skin)
1 tablespoon toasted sesame oil
1 teaspoon sugar
1 teaspoon MSG
1 recipe Basic Bao Dough (page 16)

BRING a large stockpot of salted water to a boil.

MEANWHILE, in a large bowl, make an ice bath by filling the bowl halfway with ice and covering the ice with cold water.

BLANCH the broccoli in the boiling water, without stirring, for 5 to 10 seconds, until greens become vibrant. Use a slotted spoon to carefully transfer the broccoli to the ice-water bath. Stir the broccoli in the water to make sure it is evenly cooled, then transfer to a paper towel–lined plate to drain.

ONCE the broccoli is drained and cooled, chop it into ¼-inch pieces and place in a medium bowl. Drain any excess liquid from the bowl.

HEAT 1 tablespoon of the neutral oil in a medium sauté pan. Add the bamboo shoots and cook for 2 to 3 minutes, stirring occasionally, until some color has developed. Transfer to a paper towel–lined plate to drain.

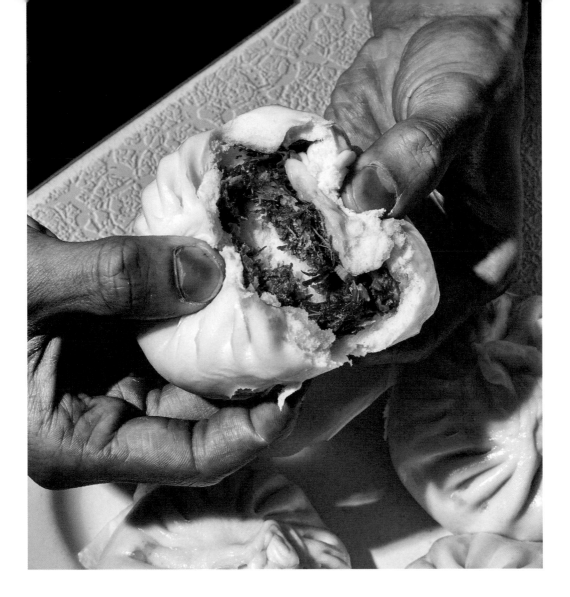

ADD the bamboo shoots to the bowl with the broccoli. Add the dried bean curd, remaining 1 tablespoon neutral oil, toasted sesame oil, sugar, salt, and MSG. Toss the contents of the bowl until fully combined. Cover and refrigerate overnight or for up to 10 hours to firm up the filling.

WHEN you're ready to use the filling, remove from the refrigerator, drain off any excess liquid, and stir. Fill the bao according to the instructions on page 17. Set up a steamer according to the instructions on page 10, add the bao, and steam for 12 to 15 minutes until bun is firm to touch with a little bit of give. Serve immediately.

THE MAN: UNCLE WALLY TANG

First things first, let's just get it out of the way that Uncle Wally isn't my *blood* uncle, any more than Big Brother Kong (Wun Gaw), the chef at Nom Wah, is really my elder sibling. Uncle, in Chinese as it is in many other cultures, is a title of respect. He's my *Tio* Wally, my *wofa* Wally, my *oncle* Wally. (Also true that Wally isn't his given name, any more than Wilson is mine. He's Tang Gum Wor; I'm Dong Wai.) Welcome to the wonderfully complicated world of logograms! It is true that Uncle Wally came from the same neighborhood called Tong On my family came from and shares our last name, but Tang is the Toisanese equivalent of Smith, and we didn't know each other back on the mainland. But Uncle Wally has been in my life as long as I can remember. And he's always been old.

Getting Uncle Wally to talk is like pulling teeth. Getting him to talk about the past is like pulling teeth from a cow. Getting him to talk about himself in the past is like pulling teeth from a crow. My biological uncle, Fred, who has known Wally forever, says he's always been quiet. Now that he's in his eighties, Wally speaks even less. He mostly watches the world move at its frantic pace—quiet brown eyes under unruly gray eyebrows, a cigarette dangling from his lips, Gary Cooper–style—from the stillness of his social club on Ludlow Street. But that doesn't mean he doesn't have a story to tell.

Today, Uncle Wally spends most of his time at the Tong On Association, a four-story building he and a bunch of other Toisanese guys bought back in the 1980s for a few thousand dollars. He hangs out on the third-floor lounge amid a vibrant hodgepodge of calendars, shopping bags, red lanterns, fake plants, boxes of Chinese snacks, and thousands of photographs tacked onto the walls. When I ask Uncle Wally to tell me about the history of Nom Wah, he grunts, "I already told you everything."

I know, Uncle Wally, I say, but I want to hear it one more time. It's for a *book*! His face remains impassive and he reaches to grab a smoke from his golden and red pack of Double Happiness cigarettes. With the reluctance of someone never asked, he begins to tell me about his life.

Wally was eleven years old when he arrived in Hong Kong from Guangzhou at the close of World War II. By that time, his parents had both died and he was left in the care of his sister, who was thirteen years old at the time. The Tang kids were part of a huge flood of Chinese immigrants fleeing to the British colony from the Nationalist-Communist civil war that had begun in 1927, died down in 1937, and then reignited at the end of World War II with terrible ferocity. Particularly for those in South China, Hong Kong was shelter from the storm. From 1945 to 1951, Hong Kong's

population exploded from 600,000 to 2.1 million. Not knowing much in the way of anything, and being smaller than the other boys but also cleverer, Wally found work in the crowded and chaotic world of Hong Kong's dim sum kitchens.

Even then Hong Kong was to dim sum what Rome is to cacio e pepe or what the South is to barbecue. Though it bore little in common with the mind-bending vertical metropolis of today, the arteries and capillaries of the city were clogged with closet-sized dim sum joints, catering to the influx of millions of mostly poor Cantonese immigrants. Wally spent his nights in a crowded flat, sleeping on the floor, and his days in the kitchen.

For five years, Wally saw little daylight. His was a hazy existence, bathed in the steam of thousands of har gow and siu mai, or the artificial daylight of the Hong Kong night. The only exceptions, of course, were the short smoke breaks allowed every couple of hours. (By age twelve, Wally was an enthusiastic and committed smoker.) Under the tutelage of chefs whose names have long evaporated, Wally learned the basics of dim sum: how to mince the shrimp for har gow, leaving just enough texture; how to grind the pork for siu mai; how to suspend char siu at that exact point of sweetness and silkiness and to turn rice flour and water into silken cheung fun. He learned the slow subtleties of steam and overcame his boyish fear of the wok's dangerous dancing flame. Later, he was taught the intricacies of folding the dumpling skins into what appeared to him impossibly delicate coin purses. One benefit of working as a child: his small, nimble fingers made his dumpling folds particularly refined.

Eventually Wally found a spot in the kitchen of a Hong Kong bakery and began to hone his long apprenticeship in moon cakes, the bite-sized intricately decorated pastries today traditionally eaten during the Mid-Autumn Festival but back then available and eaten year-round. I always thought the pastry shell of the cakes came in just two variations: either filled with red bean or lotus seed paste. But Wally snorts and shakes his head derisively. "There were many varieties, Wilson: cured Jinhua ham, Chaozhou winter melon, coconut, dried scallop moon cake, five nuts moon cakes. We made them all." Each day, the kitchen churned out thousands of these moon cakes, which were each devoured in one bite with a gulp of tea by folks just as hard-pressed as Wally, hurrying from one place to another.

By 1950, Wally had spent a third of his life in the cramped kitchens and flats of Hong Kong and the third before that desperately poor in Guangzhou. He didn't know what else was out there. The tales of America that came wafting back across the ocean had a fabulist odor. But he knew that he didn't want to spend the remainder of his life where he was, doing what he was doing. He said goodbye to his sister, his last remaining family, forged his identity papers by turning the four into a two, instantly aged two years (in other words, aged himself over eighteen), and found passage on a hulking rusty-hulled ocean tanker. Lacking funds to pay for his journey, he took work as a custodian in exchange for his passage. It was a long journey—

first to Sydney, then to London, Los Angeles, Panama, and New York—and it must have been hard, but when I press for details, Wally just fiddles with his cigarette lighter and doesn't answer. I begin to understand his silences a bit better. At a little under a hundred pounds in a multiton vessel, destined to an uncertain future written in an unknown language, of course you keep your mouth shut and eyes open.

Wally says he jumped ship in New York because of the cigarettes. "In Hong Kong," he tells me, "there were so many different options. In New York there were only two: ones without filters for twenty-two cents and ones with filters for twenty-three cents." I ask him to clarify. My Cantonese is good, but maybe I missed something. Can it really be true that he cast the die of his life based solely on the simplicity of choice between two types of cigarettes? (And, of course, in 1950, there were literally hundreds of cigarette brands from Chesterfields to Lucky Strikes being advertised on every flat surface in New York.) But he's adamant. "Two types of cigarettes. Two prices. I knew it was a good country." Whatever his reasoning, in the fall of 1950, Wally joined the wave of Chinese immigrants to the United States, disembarking somewhere in the South and taking a train to New York City. When Wally got to Penn Station, he walked south along the avenues until the street signs were written in Chinese. Though the war had prompted the US government to soften their fucked-up racist exclusion policy and allow more Chinese to enter legally, Wally came here undocumented.

It was for Wally as it has been for the millions of immigrants before him and the millions after. Success was not guaranteed, nor was survival. Nor was failure or poverty. Nothing was guaranteed. He was a man—a boy really—on his own, the guarantor of his own future. Knowing no one, owning nothing, Wally found a flat on 109 Ludlow Street, sharing the space with a bunch of other Chinese bachelors. He got a job somewhere in New Jersey washing dishes in a Chinese restaurant for $160 a month. Just as in Hong Kong, his existence was evenly split between working and sleeping, with but small remainders of minutes for smoking. (He spent the extra penny for the filtered cigarettes.) Then one day, a few weeks after his arrival, Wally missed his ride to New Jersey, had no idea how to get there, and decided to bide his time until he could figure out a way to get to New Jersey at a little tea parlor on Doyers: Nom Wah.

Even then Nom Wah was already thirty years old, and though the block itself looked much different than it does today—for instance, that concrete bunker of a post office was still an empty lot—the inside of Nom Wah was much the same: the same clank and clamor, the same well-worn welcome. Seventeen, by now at loose ends and accidentally idle, Wally sipped tea alone until May Choy, the owner of Nom Wah, struck up a conversation. May, by all accounts a woman with her wits about her, whose maternal and business instincts worked in synchronous harmony, wanted to know who Wally was, where he was from, what he had done, what he did now, and how much he got paid. When she found out he had been a dim sum cook in Hong Kong, she knew she had her man. She marched him back to the kitchen, offered him $20 more a month than he was making in New Jersey, and bade him stay.

Wally stayed at Nom Wah for the next sixty years. At first, he worked as a dishwasher. Silent, skin softened by scalding water, but watching, watching, always watching the bustle of the kitchen. What he didn't see was anyone better than he was at making dim sum. In fact, what he noticed was that no one really knew what they were doing. Like him, the rest of the kitchen staff were there because they needed work. Unlike him, they hadn't spent the last five years in the crucible of Hong Kong kitchens.

These men—for they were all men—were older than Wally and bigger too. So he knew he had to be careful in how he taught them, politic in how he navigated the kitchen hierarchy, such as it was. With as few words as possible, he began to impart the knowledge he had acquired about dim sum. That Wally wore his knowledge lightly and gave it freely soon earned him friends, including one young cook named Wun Gaw. May and Ed Choy took note of Wally too, bumping him up from dishwasher to chef in a matter of months. And so it was that Wally began to build a life for himself in America, one dumpling at a time. Paid a livable wage with a steady job, finally, he began to feel himself more firmly in the world. Through a friend, he met an American-born Chinese woman named Sok Tang Yuen. They were married in 1959 and moved into an apartment on Pike Street. With a little bit of

dough, he and a bunch of other Toisanese bought the Ludlow Street building. They furnished it with couches and tables bought at a steep discount from a Nom Wah regular who worked at Macy's.

As Wally grew into his own, the Choys gradually ceded the reins of the business. They were getting old and the restaurant, which had always skated by just above the black, had fallen into the red. By 1974, the Choys owed $30,000 to various creditors. Tired of the grind, they agreed to sell Nom Wah to Wally in exchange for the balance. And so, a quarter century after he landed in America, my Uncle Wally became the guardian of Nom Wah.

By the time I came into the picture, Wally was in his midfifties and Nom Wah was on the decline. He held on to the restaurant not as a business but as a point of pride. Nom Wah was what he had to show for his life. Nom Wah had been the engine that had helped put his children through school. Nom Wah had given him purchase in this country. It was an institution he had helped build, a small space on Earth for which he was responsible. But he had grown weary of shouldering the burden and wished, in his own quiet way, to enjoy the rest of his years at leisure.

These days, I don't see Uncle Wally too often, maybe a few times a year, for a big Lunar New Year feast he has at the association plus during the Mid-Autumn Festival. Even during those festive occasions, it would be unusual for him to be effusive, and he still isn't. But I can see how happy he is, surrounded by his own friends from the village and his years here in New York. I am just one part of that. But he figures so prominently in my own story and, of course, in the story of Nom Wah, that he's never far from my mind. When we meet in person, I'm still struck—and honestly, struggle a bit—with his abiding quiet. I can see time pulling like inverted marionette strings, tugging Wally closer to the ground. He stoops a bit more, the bags under his eyes carry more weight, but by and large he's still the same steady cipherlike Uncle Wally.

I want to ask him more about his life, about whether he has any regrets, about whether he is happy or proud or worried. But I can tell even divulging this much about himself—the scant biographical facts of eight decades and thousands of miles—has tired him out. He taps out a smoke from his golden packet of Double Happiness, lights it, takes a drag. The cherry glows, and as he exhales, the smoke surrounds him like the mist of a distant mountain.

CLOCKWISE FROM TOP: Shrimp and Chive Har Gow (p. 69);
Har Gow (p. 69); House Special Pan-Fried Pork Dumplings (p. 45);
Shrimp and Snow Pea Leaf Har Gow (p. 69)

DUMPLINGS

My first memory of dumplings wasn't at Nom Wah. It wasn't even in Chinatown. No, the first dumpling in the life of young Wilson Tang was had at some ghetto Chinese spot in Ridgewood, Queens, my mom stopped at on her way home from work. It came swimming in a crystalline broth, accompanied by a few strands of pink-tipped shredded pork and a pinch of scallions. Its skin was silky and its insides were juicy. It made me happy.

I was a latchkey kid. My mom was a working mom, moving between a few Chinese banks from Chinatrust Bank (USA) to the Abacus Bank. I got out of school at 2 p.m. and walked home with my key literally hanging around my neck. I'd chill at home, play video games, read, and wait for my mom to come. When I was lucky, on her way back from work, she'd stop at Lee's Garden on the corner of DeKalb and Wyckoff to pick up the aforementioned divine dumpling. Lee's was the kind of Chinese place that served its chow mein through a bulletproof-glass window. When Mom got home, smelling of perfume, office supplies, and Lee's, I was the happiest kid in Queens. Inside that brown paper bag wrapped—just to be shitty to the environment—in another, plastic bag were some of my favorite things: wonton soup, chicken with broccoli, and moo goo gai pan, this version with the cheap-ass canned mushrooms and water chestnuts.

Mom, wontons, and me. Those are some of my favorite memories. Since then, of course, my dumpling knowledge has grown deeper and my appreciation more subtle. Those weeknight memories now commingle with some truly transcendent dumplings, from the plump boiled pork gauu zi with Red Devil hot sauce from Southwind (sadly no longer with us) to sundry dumplings eaten around the world whose names I remember not but whose flavors still excite my tongue. Cue slo-mo montage of Wilson eating dumplings around the world set to "Tonight I Celebrate My Love for You" by Roberta Flack and Peabo Bryson.

Sitting with Wun Gaw at Nom Wah, I absorbed the ins and outs of dumpling making on an industrial scale. In our commissary kitchen, there's a $50,000 dumpling machine we bought in Taiwan that can wrap hundreds of dumplings an hour. But when I make them at home for my kids, it's still a hand operation. Now my kids join me, and the three of us repeat the same hand movements Chinese cooks have been making unbroken for millennia. There's an entire taxonomy of dumplings, from varying folds to wrapper material, not to mention a panoply of fillings.

Dumplings are nearly synonymous with dim sum, and they've earned that spot. By far, dumplings are our best seller at all of our Nom Wah locations. We go through about eight thousand per day. That's a lot of dumplings. By way of breakdown, we do a brisk business in at least four types of dumplings:

GAUU ZI: These are your go-to dumplings. Originally from Northern China, they're bite-sized packages made with a thin wheat wrapper and are very versatile. They can be steamed, in which case they emerge almost silky with a light yellow hue, or pan-fried, in which case they are darker and partially encrusted in a delicious crunchy wrapper.
WRAPPER USED: Shanghai-style circular wonton wrapper. We prefer the Twin Marquis brand.

WONTON: The line between what is a gauu zi and what is a wonton is blurry. Basically, a wonton is gauu zi made with a thinner Hong Kong–style square wrapper, instead of circular Shanghai-style ones and with a slightly different folding mechanic. Less technical in nature, the word *wonton* stems from "hundun," or primordial chaos.
WRAPPER USED: Hong Kong–style square wonton wrapper.

SIU MAI: These small dumplings are like gauu zi, if you left them in the dryer too long and the wrapper shrank like a wool sweater. Most common siu mai are pork siu mai, but we make a variety, including chicken and shrimp.
WRAPPER USED: Hong Kong–style circular wonton wrapper.

HAR GOW: Made with a translucent crystal dumpling skin and delicately folded, har gow are basically tricked-out shrimp gauu zi with a few extra folds.
WRAPPER USED: Homemade (page 69).
XIAO LONG BAO: For my money, the most impressive of all dumplings but, sadly, actually bao. These are broth-filled purses that are then steamed.
WRAPPER USED: Homemade (page 70).

HOW TO MAKE DUMPLINGS

How to make dumplings means mostly how to fold dumplings, not so much how to make the dough. At Nom Wah, like literally everywhere else, we use store-bought dumpling skins. Though I've included some recipes for dumpling skins, only masochists make their own wrappers. Don't be precious. Go buy some. We get ours from Twin Marquis, a noodle-and-wrapper company that started in Chinatown in 1989 but has since expanded to Bushwick and New Jersey and other places. Their stuff is very gettable online and always the highest quality.

As for the folding, that you have to do yourself. Folding dumplings isn't hard, but it takes practice. I'm not talking Malcolm Gladwell's 10,000-Hour Rule. Dumpling skins come in pretty large stacks. By the end of a package, you'll be as good as you'll need to be for a feast. That said, what I'd recommend is that the first time you make dumplings, double the recipe. First

dumplings are like first pancakes: wonky and uneven. Practiced dumplings are like only children: perfect, compact, punctilious creatures, labored over by loving parents who don't let their inner lives spill out to the rest of the world but present a flawless facade, all the while containing the building pressure until they *explode* with flavor and pent-up juices.

Whether you're making har gow, gauu zi, siu mai, or xiao long bao, the most important tip I can give you is don't go ham in the amount of filling you use. More isn't always better. Think of your dumplings like letters, delicious flour-based envelopes. You can't overstuff your envelope or it'll get returned to sender. Similarly, don't overstuff your dumpling or it'll break apart, spilling its filling like a thirteen-year-old, drunk on his dad's schnapps. Use a proper tablespoon, not a heaping one, not two of one, just one proper tablespoon.

Apart from the folds, as shown in the following pages; the second variable in dumpling assembly is not to be shy about smushing together the wrapper to seal the dumplings closed. Use a bit of water on your finger if need be to moisten the dough. As dumplings cook, they have a tendency to pop open. Your seam is the weakest part, so press it hard.

DUMPLING DIPPING SAUCE

MAKES 2 CUPS

The ideal accompaniment for most dumplings is this sharp and sweet sauce. The acidity cuts the rich fattiness of the filling. Do not use it sparingly. Use it with abandon.

¾ cup light soy sauce
1 cup rice wine vinegar
3½ tablespoons sugar
1 tablespoon toasted sesame oil

PLACE all ingredients in a small bowl. Whisk together until well mixed and the sugar dissolved. Dumpling Dipping Sauce can be kept covered in the refrigerator for up to three days.

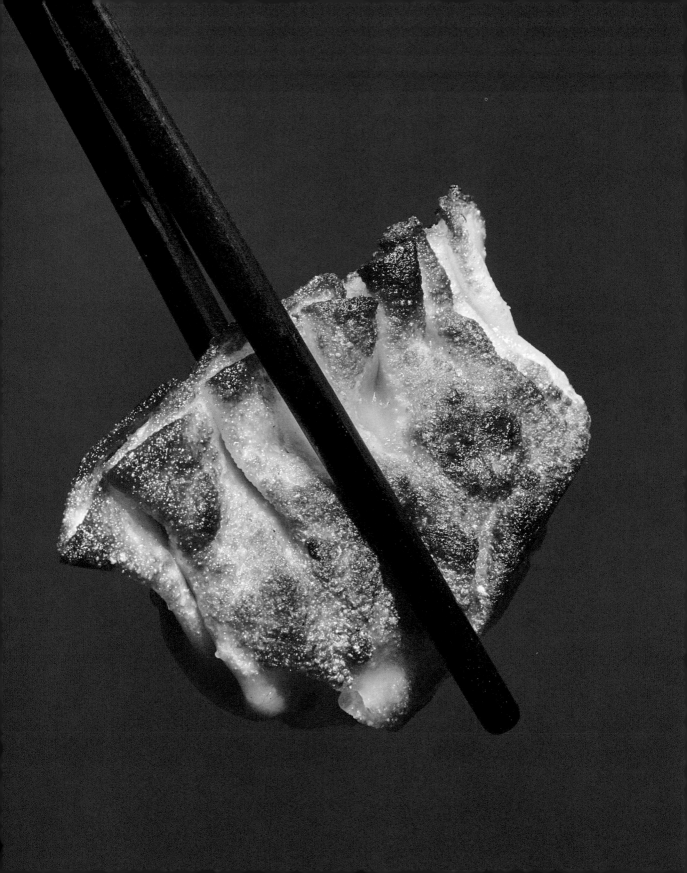

GAUU ZI

Close your eyes and think of dumplings. You'll probably think of gauu zi, small golden purses that can be had, a dozen for few dollars, at any one of the many dumpling joints across the Chinatowns of the world. In fact, gauu zi are so ubiquitous that at Nom Wah we just refer to them as dumplings.

Gauu zi originated in Northern China sometime around the Han dynasty (220–206 BC) but they've been found preserved intact in tombs across China. Originally eaten during the Lunar New Year to bring good luck—their shape vaguely recalls the silver bars then used as currency, although, let's face it, when you're poor everything looks like money—now gauu zi are eaten year-round all over the world. They're among the easiest of dumplings to make and the most versatile.

HOW TO MAKE GAUU ZI

WRAPPER: Shanghai-style circular wonton wrapper

DAMPEN a towel under which to keep the rest of the dumpling wrappers while you work.

PREPARE a parchment-lined baking sheet on which to store the already prepared dumplings.

STEP 1. Place 1½ teaspoons of filling in the center of each dumpling wrapper.

STEP 2. Fold the dumpling into a half-moon shape.

STEP 3. Hold the dumpling, seam-side up, between your thumb and index finger.

STEP 4. Use the index finger and thumb of your other hand to pinch a section of the dumpling edge and pull it toward the web of the holding hand to make a small pleat.

STEP 5. Repeat around the edge of the dumpling until you have between 6 and 8 pleats.

MAKE AHEAD: Dumplings can be kept in the refrigerator for up to four days or frozen for up to three months.

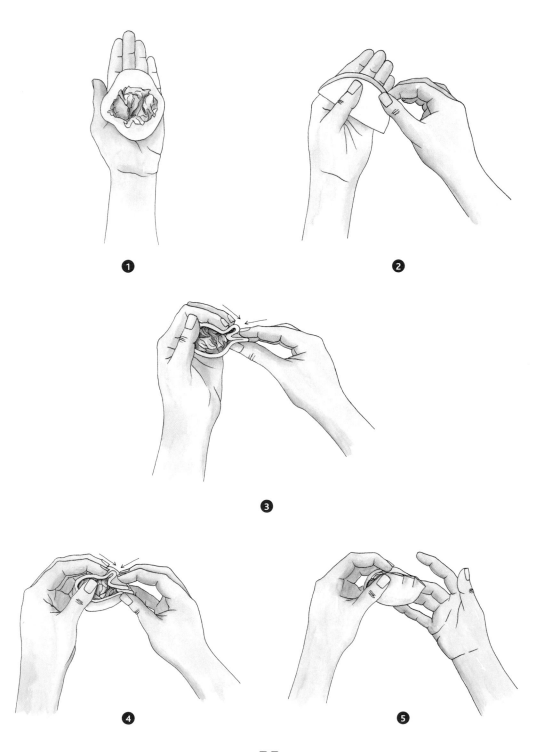

THE THREE MASTER FILLINGS

Much of dim sum is predicated on the three Master Fillings. It's time you meet them. (My friend Calvin calls these the Mother Meats, but . . . gross.)

Once you have a working knowledge of master fillings, you can start building on them. It's simple, like grammar or car wash options or Pachelbel's Canon: theme and variation. If you take the Pork Master Filling and add chives, you get pork and chive dumplings. Shrimp and snow pea leaf dumplings contain Shrimp Master Filling with snow pea shoots added. You get it.

TOP-LEFT: House Special Pan-Fried Pork Dumplings (p. 45);
BOTTOM-LEFT: Shrimp and Chive Har Gow (p. 69)

PORK MASTER FILLING

MAKES FILLING FOR 20 DUMPLINGS

Pork Master Filling is the spiritual center of dumplings. It is contained in the heart of many dumplings, like magic in the finger of *Willow*. It gives that good good dim sum flavor. It is made primarily of pork. And, therefore, it is known as the Pork Master Filling. Pity the pig—easily kept, cheaply fed, and delicious—for these characteristics have made it a staple in Chinese cooking from Neolithic times to the present. When Uncle Wally throws down at Tong On Association, it's the whole suckling pig, borne by four guys on its platter, that comes out of the kitchen. When I shut down the restaurant and take everyone out for karaoke and dinner, we're eating pork. Pig makes the party at Nom Wah too, though more often than not it comes in filling form.

This filling isn't, of course, *just* pork. In the Chinese pantry, pork has a best amigo: shrimp. Shrimp is like the Amos to Pork's Boris. Shrimp is the Piggie to the Pork's Elephant. And it's easy to see why. Like pigs, shrimp are easy to raise, easy to catch, easy to feed, and delicious. Guangzhou cuisine is full of shrimp, presented in an astonishing array: there is shrimp paste, whole shrimp, shrimp powder, shrimp chopped up and rolled into balls, shrimp—as is here the case—as pork wingman.

Pork Master Filling also has a bunch of other delicious things in it, like chicken powder and dried shiitake mushrooms (dung gu). The former endows the filling with Ineffable Chicken Presence. The latter gives the filling body, texture, and, because the mushrooms are smoked before they're dried, a wonderful burst of umami.

3 dried shiitake mushrooms
10 ounces pork collar, roughly chopped
8 ounces small shrimp, peeled and roughly chopped
1 teaspoon kosher salt
1½ teaspoons sugar
1 tablespoon chicken powder
¼ teaspoon ground white pepper
1 teaspoon cornstarch
1 teaspoon toasted sesame oil

SOAK the mushrooms in hot water for 20 to 30 minutes, until tender.

REMOVE, pat dry, then roughly chop. Combine all the ingredients in a bowl and stir well to incorporate.

MAKE AHEAD: The filling can be kept refrigerated for up to 3 days or frozen for 3 months.

SHRIMP MASTER FILLING

MAKES FILLING FOR 20 DUMPLINGS

Now, not everyone eats pork. For them we have two declensions of Pork Master Filling, each with their individual charms. The first, Shrimp Master Filling, replaces the pork with cuttlefish. (Cuttlefish is the pork of the ocean.) The result is a wonderfully oceanic but not at all fish-fishy flavor with a unique flavor that is synonymous with dim sum.

4 ounces cuttlefish or squid, roughly chopped
8 ounces small whole shrimp, peeled
1 tablespoon neutral oil
¼ teaspoon ground white pepper
1 teaspoon toasted sesame oil
¼ teaspoon salt
1 teaspoon sugar
1 tablespoon chicken powder
2 tablespoons potato starch

COMBINE all the ingredients in a blender. Blend at high speed until sticky like grout or a paste, 3 to 5 minutes, stopping to scrape the sides of the machine as needed. Overblending the mixture will result in a filling with no chew. And chew is a good thing.

MAKE AHEAD: The filling can be kept refrigerated for up to 3 days or frozen for 3 months.

NO PORK NO SHRIMP MASTER FILLING

MAKES FILLING FOR 20 DUMPLINGS

No Pork No Shrimp Master Filling is another way of saying vegetarian filling. It draws its body from a pantry of woodland flora, including bamboo shoots, shiitake mushrooms, wood ear mushrooms, and a bunch of cabbage. Unlike the other fillings, which use entirely raw ingredients, you'll need to quickly stir-fry the vegetables before making the filling. The result is a startlingly fresh and wholesome filling that is both satisfying and doesn't make you want to take a nap immediately after.

2 ounces dried wood ear mushrooms
2 teaspoons neutral oil
8 ounces medium yellow napa cabbage (about ¼ cabbage), shredded
4 fresh shiitake mushrooms, diced
1 small carrot, diced
¼ cup bamboo shoots, chopped
1 teaspoon sugar
1 teaspoon white pepper
1 teaspoon Shaoxing wine
½ teaspoon toasted sesame oil
1 teaspoon cornstarch

SOAK mushrooms in hot water for 20 to 30 minutes, until tender. Remove, pat dry, and roughly chop.

HEAT the neutral oil in a wok or a large heavy skillet over high heat until hot but not smoking. Add the cabbage, mushrooms, carrot, and bamboo shoots and cook for 30 seconds to 1 minute. Add the sugar, white pepper, Shaoxing wine, and toasted sesame oil and toss for 30 seconds, or until the vegetables are beginning to soften. Add the cornstarch and toss once more to incorporate it. Cool completely before using.

MAKE AHEAD: The filling can be kept refrigerated for up to 3 days or frozen for 3 months.

HOUSE SPECIAL PAN-FRIED PORK DUMPLINGS

MAKES 20 DUMPLINGS

These are our archetypal dumplings and one of the most popular orders across the Nom Wah universe. There's really no mystery as to why: dumplings are delicious. To the extent that ours are special—and they are because it's in the name—it's due less to the dumpling form and to the Pork Master Filling. Shrimp and Pork are like the Cardi B and Offset or Kanye and Kim of dumpling filling: a sexy, deeply compatible, and wholly enviable partnership.

1 recipe Pork Master Filling (page 41)
20 Shanghai-style circular wrappers
2 tablespoons neutral oil
Dumpling Dipping Sauce (page 35) for serving

MAKE the dumplings according to the Gauu Zi method (see page 38).

SET up a steamer following the instructions on page 10. Working in batches, add the dumplings, making sure to leave 1½ inches of space between each (they expand as they cook), and steam for for 12 to 13 minutes. Let rest for a minute or so to tighten slightly.

HEAT the neutral oil in a large nonstick pan over medium-high heat. Working in batches, add the dumplings, pleat to the side, and pan-fry until golden brown, approximately 1 minute per side.

SERVE with Dumpling Dipping Sauce.

PAN-FRIED CHICKEN AND CABBAGE DUMPLINGS

MAKES 20 DUMPLINGS

Chicken is like pork that can fly. It is much lighter both as animal and as protein and also healthier. Among our best sellers at Nom Wah are these chicken and cabbage dumplings. The chicken gives these guys body while the cabbage gives them volume.

10 ounces skinless chicken breast, finely chopped

6 ounces medium yellow napa cabbage (approximately ⅕ cabbage), shredded

2 slices fresh ginger, ⅛ to ¼ inch thick, diced

2 scallions, finely chopped

1 teaspoon salt

1½ teaspoons sugar

1 tablespoon chicken powder

¼ teaspoon ground white pepper

1 teaspoon cornstarch

1 teaspoon toasted sesame oil

20 Shanghai-style circular wrappers

2 tablespoons neutral oil

Dumpling Dipping Sauce (page 35) for serving

IN a large bowl, mix together the chicken, cabbage, ginger, and scallions until the mixture resembles a fine paste. Add the salt, sugar, chicken powder, white pepper, cornstarch, and toasted sesame oil and continue to stir for 3 to 5 minutes, until well incorporated.

MAKE the dumplings according to the Gauu Zi method (see page 38).

SET up a steamer following the instructions on page 10. Working in batches, add the dumplings, making sure to leave 1½ inches of space between each (they expand as they cook), and steam for 12 to 13 minutes. Let rest for a minute or so to tighten slightly.

HEAT the neutral oil in a large nonstick pan over medium-high heat. Working in batches, add the dumplings, pleat to the side, and pan-fry until golden brown, approximately 1 minute per side.

SERVE with Dumpling Dipping Sauce.

EDAMAME DUMPLINGS

MAKES 20 DUMPLINGS

In meat dumplings, the meat is a binding agent. In veggie dumplings, there is no meat, and man, are they a drag to fold, the dumpling equivalent of herding cats. The filling simply doesn't adhere. After lots of frustrated attempts at wrapping, Julie Cole, our chef at Nolita, developed this recipe. The blitzed edamame beans, fortified with xanthan gum, give the filling its body, but if you happen *not* to have xanthan gum lying around, you can forgo it, although the filling will be slightly less cohesive, or substitute with cornstarch.

MAKE AHEAD: *The filling must be prepared the day before you make the dumplings.*

10½ ounces shelled frozen edamame beans, defrosted

3½ tablespoons finely chopped fresh Chinese chives

2 teaspoons kosher salt

7 ounces drained canned straw mushrooms

½ ounce dry vermicelli noodles, hydrated in hot water for 10 minutes and drained

1 tablespoon sugar

¼ teaspoon xanthan gum (or substitute an equal amount cornstarch)

1½ teaspoons toasted sesame oil

3 tablespoons Szechuan chili oil

20 round spinach dumpling wrappers (we use Twin Marquis)

Dumpling Dipping Sauce (page 35) for serving

TO MAKE THE FILLING:

PUT the edamame beans in a food processor and pulse 2 to 3 times for a very large rough chop. Transfer to a bowl.

PUT the chives in a microwave-safe bowl, add ½ teaspoon of the salt, and stir to combine. Microwave for 30 seconds until warm. Wrap the heated chives in a kitchen towel and twist and squeeze the liquid out over the sink. Add the chives to the chopped edamame beans and mix to combine.

ADD the straw mushrooms to the food processor and pulse 2 to 3 times for a very large rough chop. Transfer to another bowl.

ROUGHLY chop the vermicelli noodles, add them to the bowl of mushrooms, and mix to combine.

TRANSFER the edamame-chive and mushroom-vermicelli mixtures to separate strainers set over bowls. Cover each with paper towels and use any type of weight (such as a soup can) to weigh each mixture down. The weight should be something that covers the entire mixture, not a small can that covers only ¼ of it. Liquid will only strain out of the portion that is compressed, so it all needs to be weighed down. Refrigerate for at least 10 hours and up to 24 hours.

REMOVE the mixtures from the refrigerator. Add half of the edamame-chive mixture to the mushroom-vermicelli mixture.

IN a food processor, combine the sugar, xanthan gum (or cornstarch), sesame oil, and remaining salt and process for 2 minutes until well incorporated. Add the remaining edamame-chive mixture and the chili oil. Process until the mixture forms a smooth paste.

ADD the paste to the bowl with the edamame, chives, mushrooms, and vermicelli. Mix the filling until very well combined.

TO ASSEMBLE AND COOK THE DUMPLINGS:
MAKE the dumplings according to the Gauu Zi method (see page 38).

SET up a steamer following the instructions on page 10. Working in batches, add the dumplings, making sure to leave 1½ inches of space between each (they expand as they cook), and steam for 6 minutes until dumpling is glossy. Serve immediately, with Dumpling Dipping Sauce if desired.

EDAMAME DUMPLINGS IN SOUP

SERVES 4

FOR THE BROTH:

1 large Spanish onion, washed

1 (2-inch) piece fresh ginger

2 carrots, medium, washed and cut into
1-inch slices

1 medium daikon (about 4 ounces), cut into
1-inch slices

2 sheets of dashi kombu (dried seaweed)

1 small bunch fresh cilantro

4 scallions, rinsed and dried

2 cloves garlic, smashed with the side of a
knife

1 gram whole star anise, roughly ½ pod

4½ teaspoons mushroom powder

¼ teaspoon kosher salt

1 tablespoon light soy sauce

1½ teaspoons rice wine vinegar

6¼ cups cold water

FOR THE SOUP:

1 pound yu choy (also known as edible
rape) or other Chinese green, thick stems
peeled and trimmed

16 Edamame Dumplings (page 49)

2 scallions, thinly sliced on the bias

TO MAKE THE BROTH:

SLICE the onion and ginger in half
lengthwise. Place the onion and ginger
directly on a gas burner over a high flame,
peeled side down, and burn them until the
flesh side is completely black. Flip and do the
same on the skin side. (If you do not have a
gas stovetop, you can do this over high heat
in a well-oiled skillet.)

REMOVE the onion and ginger to a large
pot. Add the remaining ingredients. Bring
to a boil over high heat, then lower the heat
to low and cook, uncovered, at a very light
simmer for 2 hours.

TURN off the heat and strain through a
chinois or very fine strainer. The broth is
ready to use for soup.

TO MAKE THE SOUP:

HEAT the strained broth in a large pot. Add
the yu choy and cook for 2 minutes, or until
just softened. Divide the soup equally among
4 bowls. Add the edamame dumplings and
garnish with the sliced scallions.

FROM LEFT TO RIGHT: Triple C (Chinese Chopped Cheese)
Dumplings (p. 58); Sweet Potato Kale Wontons (p. 54);
Chorizo Potato Dumplings with Dill Chimichurri Sauce (p. 56)

SWEET POTATO KALE WONTONS

MAKES 20 WONTONS

Now is a great time to talk about Calvin Eng, the young and impossibly handsome chef who opened Nom Wah Nolita with us. Like many of my friends, I met Calvin on Instagram. I don't know who DM'd whom first, but we slid into each other's lives like a letter into an envelope. Calvin grew up in Bay Ridge, the son of Toisanese immigrants. He's younger than I am, but we had very similar experiences growing up, getting dragged by his parents to Chinatown on the weekends to shop, go to Chinese school, and visit relatives. When I met Cal, he was only twenty-one, freshly graduated from Johnson & Wales University. But he was fiercely ambitious, and when we opened Nom Wah Nolita, I knew he was the guy I wanted at the helm. Cal immediately began taking traditional dim sum and putting his twist on it. A great example is this vegan dumpling, which, unlike many vegan foods, is exceptionally flavorful. The result is a marriage between a pierogi and a gauu zi and heralded tremendous things for Nom Wah Nolita.

1 tablespoon kosher salt, plus more for boiling the sweet potatoes

2 pounds sweet potatoes

4 ounces kale, stems removed, leaves cut into thin ribbons

3 tablespoons minced fresh ginger

3 cloves garlic, minced

¼ cup thinly sliced scallions

3 tablespoons light soy sauce

1 tablespoon toasted sesame oil

1 tablespoon garlic powder

2 teaspoons ground white pepper

20 Hong Kong–style square wonton wrappers

Dumpling Dipping Sauce (page 35) for serving

TO MAKE THE FILLING:

BRING a large pot of cold salted water to a boil. Add the sweet potatoes and cook for approximately 15 minutes, until they can be easily pierced with a fork. Allow to cool slightly, then carefully remove the skins from the sweet potatoes.

IN a large bowl, combine the still-warm sweet potatoes, the kale, ginger, garlic, scallions, soy sauce, toasted sesame oil, garlic powder, salt, and white pepper. Using a potato masher, gently mash the ingredients to make a filling, leaving some small chunks. Allow to cool completely.

TO ASSEMBLE THE WONTONS:

PLACE a wonton wrapper on a clean cutting board. Place 1 teaspoon of the filling in the middle of the wrapper. Form the filling into a rectangular shape, parallel to the wrapper. Dab the edges with water and fold the wrapper in half. Gently press the wonton to remove any air between wrapper and filling. Wet the bottom of the left corner of the wrapper. Hold both corners of the wrapper and fold them to the center. Press to seal. Repeat with the remaining wrappers and filling.

PLACE dumplings on a parchment-lined baking sheet and cover with a damp kitchen towel when completed.

SET up a steamer according to the instructions on page 10 and steam for 6 minutes. Serve immediately, with Dumpling Dipping Sauce, if desired.

CHORIZO POTATO DUMPLINGS WITH DILL CHIMICHURRI SAUCE

MAKES 20 DUMPLINGS

When we opened Nom Wah Nolita in 2016, I chose the space carefully. Not only is it a highly trafficked block just off the Bowery but the restaurant adjacent to a then-vacant corner space whose lease I also took over. The two spaces are connected by an interior hallway. Why am I talking about this again? Oh, yeah. It's because this allowed us to rent out one space for parties and events and cater from the other. And the reason that *this* piece of information matters is because one of the parties we hosted was for Adidas, which was celebrating their sponsorship of a bunch of Argentinean skateboarders. They asked Calvin to come up with some Argentinean-inspired recipes. Calvin, being a Toisanese kid from Bay Ridge, knew next to nothing about Argentinean food, but he did know how to Google. So hats off to the SEO optimization of chimichurri and chorizo, the two results that came up first in his online searches. Luckily for us, the result was insanely delicious, like an empanada that does dumplings on the DL.

FOR THE FILLING:
2 tablespoons salt, plus more for cooking the potatoes
1½ pounds red bliss or other red-skinned potatoes, diced
8 ounces raw Mexican chorizo
2 tablespoons olive oil
1 cup diced yellow onion, from approximately 1 large onion
1 tablespoon ground black pepper

FOR MAKING THE DUMPLINGS:
20 Shanghai-style dumpling wrappers
2 tablespoons neutral oil

FOR THE DILL CHIMICHURRI SAUCE:
1 shallot, minced
5 cloves garlic, minced
½ cup red wine vinegar
2 teaspoons salt
1 teaspoon ground black pepper
½ cup chopped fresh cilantro
½ cup chopped fresh flat-leaf parsley
½ cup chopped fresh dill
3 tablespoons chopped fresh oregano
¾ cup olive oil

FOR THE GARNISH:
Queso fresco, torn into small chunks

TO MAKE THE FILLING:

PUT the potatoes in a pot of cold salted water. Bring to a boil, uncovered, over high heat. Lower the heat a little and boil for approximately 15 minutes, until fork tender. Drain and place in a large bowl.

MEANWHILE, remove the casing from the chorizo and break it up into crumbles by hand.

HEAT the olive oil in a large cast-iron skillet over medium-high heat until shimmering. Add the chorizo and brown for approximately 7 minutes (do not stir until you begin to see the fat render, then stir occasionally). Add the onions and cook for an additional 3 to 4 minutes, until chorizo is crispy and onions translucent, stirring occasionally and scraping up the browned bits of chorizo.

ADD the chorizo and onions to the bowl of potatoes along with the salt and pepper.

USING a potato masher, gently mash the ingredients to make a filling, leaving some small chunks. Allow to cool completely.

TO MAKE THE DUMPLINGS:

FILL the wrappers using the Gauu Zi method (see page 38). Set up a steamer according to the instructions on page 10 Steam the dumplings for 6 minutes, until dumpling skin is glossy, then pan-fry the dumplings according to the instructions on page 11.

TO MAKE THE DILL CHIMICHURRI SAUCE AND SERVE:

WHILE the dumplings are steaming, combine all the ingredients except the olive oil in a medium bowl. Slowly stream the olive oil into the sauce, whisking until everything comes together. Serve the dumplings with the sauce and crumbled queso fresco on the side.

TRIPLE C (CHINESE CHOPPED CHEESE) DUMPLINGS
MAKES 20 DUMPLINGS

This is another one of Calvin's ingenious gauu zi collaborations with Adidas. This time the shoe company was celebrating a bunch of Bronx-born skateboarders and asked Cal to come up with an appropriate accompaniment in dumpling form. In addition to hip-hop, the Bronx is the ancestral home of the chopped cheese sandwich, a bodega-born hybrid of cheeseburger and cheesesteak. (Though purists note that the sandwich was most likely born at Hajji's in East Harlem.) Cal grew up working in a deli in Park Slope—shout-out to Doleh Supermarket on 8th Avenue—and knew his way around chopped cheese. What I love about these dumplings is that they really showcase the crazy flexibility of the form. Also, just like chopped cheese eaten drunkenly at 2 a.m. in the strangely harsh lights of a bodega, they are bone-warming, soul-saving, mouth-pleasing, and mind-blowingly delicious.

FOR THE FILLING:
1 pound ground beef
6 slices American cheese, diced
1 cup diced yellow onion, approximately
1 medium onion
1 tablespoon kosher salt
2 teaspoons ground black pepper
2 tablespoons neutral oil

FOR MAKING THE DUMPLINGS:
20 Shanghai-style dumpling wrappers
2 tablespoons neutral oil

FOR THE SAUCE:
½ cup mayonnaise
1 tablespoon ketchup
1 teaspoon Dijon mustard

FOR THE GARNISHES:
1 cup very thinly sliced iceberg lettuce
½ cup cherry tomatoes, sliced into thin rounds
¼ cup pickles, thinly sliced

TO MAKE THE FILLING:

IN a large bowl, combine ground beef, cheese, onions, salt, and pepper.

HEAT a large cast-iron skillet (or flat-top grill, if you have one) over medium-high heat. Add the neutral oil and heat until shimmering. Transfer half of the filling into the skillet, reserving the other half. Cook, breaking up the meat with a wooden spoon or spatula, until the meat is deeply browned, 2 to 3 minutes.

REMOVE from the heat, allow the mixture to cool completely, then add to the bowl with the raw ingredients, mixing well.

NOTE: *The raw meat provides the texture needed to mold the filling into the dumplings, while the cooked meat provides the flavors. If you were only using cooked meat, the texture of the filling would be too crumbly and the dumplings would fall apart when you bite into them.*

TO MAKE THE DUMPLINGS:

FILL the wrappers using the Gauu Zi method (see page 38). Set up a steamer according to the instructions on page 10. Steam the dumplings for 6 to 8 minutes, until dumpling skin is glossy, then pan-fry the dumplings according to the instructions on page 11.

TO MAKE THE SAUCE AND GARNISHES:

WHILE the dumplings are steaming, in a small bowl, combine the mayonnaise, ketchup, and mustard until it's a lovely shade of pink. Serve with the dumplings, with the garnishes on the side.

SIU MAI

What differentiates these dumplings from gauu zi is not only the size—smaller—but the wrappers, which are thinner and a darker yellow hue than the Shanghai-style wrappers used for soup dumplings and gauu zi. The word *siu mai* is a derivation of Shaoxi, which alludes to the origin of these dumplings. They were transported from their home in Hohhot, Inner Mongolia, to Ghangzhou by Shaoxi traders. Over the years, Shaoxi became siu mai. From then, because siu mai are so delicious, their popularity has spread, and they have become as numerous as stars in the sky. Derivations are found in the shumai in Japan, xiu mai in Vietnam, and siomay in Indonesia.

HOW TO MAKE SIU MAI

TYPE OF WRAPPER: Hong Kong–style circular wonton wrapper

STEP 1. Place 1 teaspoon of your filling in the center of the siu mai wrapper. Gently spread the filling in an even layer, leaving an ⅛-inch buffer.

STEPS 2 & 3. Holding the now-laden wrapper in the palm of one hand, using a butter knife, gently push the edge up to form a pleat while exerting pressure with the palm of the holding hand and your thumb so the wrapper stays cupped.

STEP 4. While maintaining that pressure, work your way around the dumpling until it looks like a beautifully filled cup with approximately 6 folds.

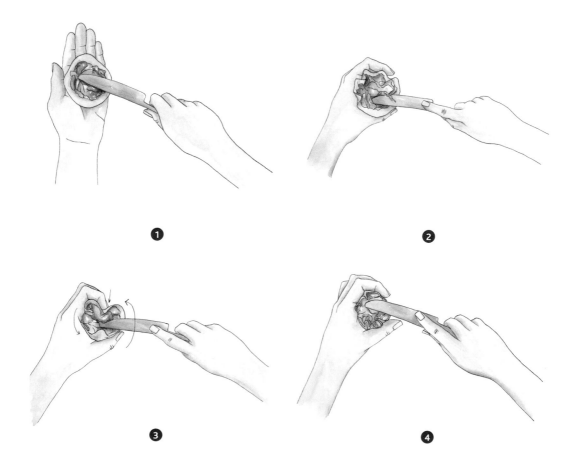

❶

❷

❸

❹

CHICKEN SIU MAI

MAKES 20 DUMPLINGS

3 fresh shiitake mushrooms (or use dried and rehydrate in hot water for 15 minutes), roughly chopped
1½ pounds boneless, skinless chicken thighs, diced
1 teaspoon salt
1½ teaspoons sugar
1 tablespoon chicken powder
¼ teaspoon ground white pepper
1 teaspoon cornstarch
1 teaspoon toasted sesame oil
20 Hong Kong–style circular wonton wrappers
Dumpling Dipping Sauce (page 35) for serving

COMBINE all the filling ingredients in a large bowl. Stir everything in one direction until it resembles a fine paste, 3 to 5 minutes.

ASSEMBLE the siu mai according to the instructions on page 62. Set up a steamer according to the instructions on page 10 and steam for 7 minutes until dumpling skin is glossy. Serve immediately, with dipping sauce if desired.

CLOCKWISE FROM TOP: Pork Siu Mai (p. 65); Chicken Siu Mai (p. 63); Shrimp Siu Mai (p. 65)

SHRIMP SIU MAI

MAKES 20 DUMPLINGS

8 ounces raw shrimp, peeled, deveined, and patted dry, roughly chopped
1 tablespoon neutral oil
¼ teaspoon ground white pepper
1 teaspoon toasted sesame oil
¼ teaspoon salt
1 teaspoon sugar
1 tablespoon chicken powder
20 Hong Kong–style circular wonton wrappers
Dumpling Dipping Sauce (page 35) for serving

COMBINE all the filling ingredients in a large bowl. Stir everything in one direction until it resembles a fine paste, 3 to 5 minutes.

ASSEMBLE the siu mai according to the instructions on page 62.

SET up a steamer according to the instructions on page 10 and steam for 7 minutes until dumpling skin is glossy. Serve immediately, with dipping sauce if desired.

PORK SIU MAI

MAKES 20 DUMPLINGS

1 recipe Pork Master Filling (page 41)
20 Hong Kong–style circular wonton wrappers
Dumpling Dipping Sauce (page 35) for serving

ASSEMBLE the siu mai according to the instructions on page 62.

SET up a steamer according to the instructions on page 10 and steam for 7 minutes until dumpling skin is glossy. Serve immediately, with dipping sauce if desired.

HAR GOW

Pretty much everyone who walks through the door at Nom Wah orders the har gow—the shrimp dumplings. They're like the pastrami sandwich at Katz's. Shrimp dumplings are the quintessential measure of dim sum. When it comes to har gow, a restaurant's caliber is judged on how thin the dumpling wrapper is and how many folds join the wrapper together. The more folds, the higher the quality of the kitchen and the more dexterous the dumpling maker. Dumpling folds are like thread counts in suits but better, because dumplings are more delicious than suits.

Back in the day, we used to make all our dumplings by hand. We'd get eight, ten, even twelve pleats into each dumpling. But it was a laborious process. Making dumplings is traditionally a two-person operation. You have the person who rolls out the dough using the side of a cleaver to press it paper-thin and the person who spoons the filling in and folds. The two work in tandem and fast, since once the dough is rolled out it quickly dries and becomes brittle. We started off that way, but we do crazy volume these days, so a few years ago I dropped 50 Gs on a fancy automatic dumpling-wrapping machine. Now our pleats are molded. Some might call that cheating; I call it innovation.

For most of our dumplings, I recommend buying premade wrappers, but har gow is different. The wrappers are so delicate and thin that we haven't been able to find a better solution than making the wrappers from scratch. The trick to achieving the crystal skin is using scalding hot water, which allows the starches to dissolve nearly completely.

CLOCKWISE FROM TOP: Shrimp and Chive Har Gow (p. 69);
Har Gow (p. 69); Shrimp and Snow Pea Leaf Har Gow (p. 69)

HAR GOW
MAKES 20 DUMPLINGS

FOR THE FILLING:
8 ounces raw shrimp, peeled, deveined, and patted dry, roughly chopped
1 tablespoon neutral oil
¼ teaspoon ground white pepper
1 teaspoon toasted sesame oil
¼ teaspoon salt
1 teaspoon sugar
1 teaspoon chicken powder

FOR THE DOUGH:
1 cup wheat starch (or potato starch)
½ cup cornstarch (or tapioca starch)
3 teaspoons lard (or a neutral oil)
1¼ cups water

TO MAKE THE FILLING:

MIX all the filling ingredients in a large bowl, stirring in one direction for 3 to 5 minutes, until the mixture starts to look and feel sticky. Cover and refrigerate for at least 1 hour while you prepare the dough.

TO MAKE THE DOUGH:

SIFT the wheat starch (or potato starch) and cornstarch (or tapioca starch) into a large bowl.

IN a medium saucepan, bring 1¼ cups water to a boil over medium-high heat and slowly pour it into the starch mixture, stirring rapidly with chopsticks. Add the lard (or neutral oil) and continue to stir with chopsticks until a loose dough ball forms.

TURN the dough out of the bowl onto a clean counter or work surface. Knead the dough by hand for a couple of minutes, until the dough has formed a smooth ball and feels uniform and elastic.

ROLL the dough into a cylinder about 3 inches thick and 1½ to 2 feet long and divide it into 20 equal pieces. Form the pieces into balls. Working quickly and using your hand, flatten each ball into circles about 3 inches in diameter. Cover the dough pieces with a damp paper towel as you make them.

ADD 1½ teaspoons of filling to each circle and fold the dumplings according to the Gauu Zi method (page 38).

SET up a steamer following the instructions on page 10. Working in batches, add the dumplings to the steamer and steam for 6 minutes, until dumpling skin is glossy. Serve immediately.

MAKE AHEAD: The filling can be kept refrigerated for up to 3 days or frozen for 3 months.

VARIATIONS:
SHRIMP AND CHIVE HAR GOW
Mix 2 ounces chopped chives into the filling.

SHRIMP AND SNOW PEA LEAF HAR GOW
Same as above but substitute roughly chopped snow pea leaves for the chives. Duh.

SHANGHAINESE SOUP DUMPLINGS (XIAO LONG BAO)

MAKES 36 SOUP DUMPLINGS

When as a kid I realized how soup dumplings were made, it felt like a cosmic mystery had been solved. The soup, though liquid at the time of serving, is solid at the time of wrapping. My mind was blown, and I filed this knowledge away as surely applicable for some life lesson later on . . . I'm still waiting to apply it. These dumplings are high in the dim sum pantheon and are originally from Jiangsu, a region north of Shanghai, hence the name. Though they fall into the genus of dumplings, they are actually bao, and the same technique (see page 17) is used to enclose them.

Just as important as mastering the making of xiao long bao, which you'll frequently find referred to as XLB, is mastering the eating of them. Every day I see diners at Nom Wah lose their precious pork broth by improper technique. The right way to eat XLB is first to grasp the dumpling by the nipple, then dip the dumpling, unbroken, into the sauce. Then gently cup the dumpling on a soup spoon before piercing the skin with tooth or chopstick to allow the juices to escape into the bowl of the spoon. Then you eat the soup dumpling and your eyes close as the rich, fatty pork broth fills your mouth. Then you repeat this until you can't eat any more and have to go take a nap.

FOR THE GELATIN CUBES:
4 tablespoons gelatin powder
2 cups chicken broth

FOR THE DOUGH:
2 cups all-purpose flour
¾ cup warm water

FOR THE FILLING:
2 pounds ground pork (70% lean)
¼ cup Shaoxing wine
1½ teaspoons salt

1 teaspoon toasted sesame oil
1½ teaspoons sugar
2 tablespoons light soy sauce
¼ teaspoon ground white pepper
3 slices fresh ginger, ⅛ to ¼ inch thick, minced
2 cups traditional gelatin cubes (see above)

FOR THE DIPPING SAUCE:
1½ cups Chinese black vinegar
5 slices fresh ginger, ⅛ to ¼ inch thick, julienned

TO MAKE GELATIN CUBES:

HEAT the chicken broth in a pot on medium-low heat. Slowly add the gelatin powder, stirring until fully dissolved.

TURN off the heat and transfer mixture into a pan or rectangular container. Once the liquid has completely cooled, cover and refrigerate from 6 hours to overnight. It will have the consistency of a firm jelly.

WHEN ready to use, turn out the gelatin onto a cutting board and cut into ⅛-inch cubes.

TO MAKE THE DOUGH:

IN a large bowl, slowly combine the flour and warm water 1 tablespoon at a time. Knead dough by hand for 7 to 10 minutes, until it is very soft and smooth. Cover with a damp cloth and let rest for 30 minutes.

TO MAKE THE FILLING:

PUT the ground pork in a food processor and pulse until it has a paste-like texture, roughly 1 minute. Transfer the pork to a bowl along with the remaining filling ingredients. Mix everything together thoroughly for about 2 minutes, until the mixture looks like a paste without any clumps. Gently fold the gelatin cubes into the mixture, being careful not to break the cubes. Cover and transfer the filling to the refrigerator until you are ready to make the dumplings. If wrapping immediately, put the filling in the freezer for 15 minutes to firm up.

TO MAKE THE DIPPING SAUCE:

IN a small bowl, mix together the black vinegar and ginger.

TO MAKE THE SOUP DUMPLINGS:

ROLL the dough into a 1¼-inch-wide log and cut off ½-ounce segments, each about the size of a pinball. Keep the dough under a damp cloth as you make your soup dumplings.

TO make each wrapper, roll the dough into a smooth ball between your hands, then place on a well-floured surface. Roll out as thinly as possible into discs about 3 inches in diameter. (You can use a cookie cutter if you want your XLB to be perfect.)

FILL each soup dumpling with 1 to 1½ teaspoons of filling. As I said earlier, xiao long bao are more bao than dumpling, which means you should use the bao method of closure (see page 17).

SET up a steamer following the instructions on page 10. Working in batches, add the soup dumplings to the steamer, making sure they are not touching, and steam for about 8 minutes or until dumpling skin is glossy. Serve immediately with the dipping sauce. I mean, stat. These have to be eaten so hot they burn your mouth.

FRIED WU GOK

MAKES 24 PIECES

Raw taro (芋頭) looks like the unfriendly love child of a coconut and a potato. But this root vegetable is one of the most versatile starches on the planet. The Hawaiians call it *kalo* and use it to make poi. It is used across West Africa and much of the southern hemisphere. Originally from Malaysia, taro has long been a staple throughout China. It's used for everything from dumplings to casseroles to bubble tea. Here, its ability to crisp into a frizzy, almost bird's-nest-like tangle is put to good use in this traditional dim sum. As you've probably noticed, for most dumpling wrappers I just say get thee to Twin Marquis—but in this case, it's worth the extra effort to make the taro wrapper from scratch.

FOR THE FILLING:
2½ teaspoons cornstarch
1 tablespoon water
½ teaspoon salt (more as needed)
½ teaspoon chicken bouillon (more as needed)
¼ teaspoon sugar
1 teaspoon Shaoxing wine
5 ounces ground pork (70% lean)
3 large dried shiitake mushrooms
2 teaspoons neutral oil
5 ounces fresh shrimp, peeled, deveined, and finely diced
1 scallion, finely diced
2 cloves garlic, finely diced
½ teaspoon Chinese five-spice powder
1 teaspoon dark soy sauce
1 teaspoon cornstarch
½ teaspoon toasted sesame oil

FOR THE WRAPPERS:
1½ pounds taro root
8 tablespoons wheat starch
¾ cup boiling (must be boiling!) water

8 tablespoons lard
1 teaspoon baking soda
½ teaspoon salt
1 tablespoon sugar
Neutral oil for deep frying

TO START THE FILLING:
IN a small bowl, mix 1½ teaspoons of the cornstarch with 1 tablespoon water. In a large bowl, combine the salt, chicken bouillon, sugar, Shaoxing wine, and cornstarch-water mixture. Add the pork and stir to coat evenly with the marinade. Refrigerate for at least 15 minutes and up to 24 hours.

TO START THE WRAPPERS:
PEEL the taro and cut it into ¾-inch slices. Set up a steamer following the instructions on page 10. Cover and steam the taro for 30 minutes, or until the slices are soft. Place the steamed taro in a bowl and mash until it becomes a paste.

73

TO FINISH THE FILLING:

WHILE the taro is steaming, continue making the filling. Submerge mushrooms in hot water for 20 to 30 minutes until tender. Remove, drain, and dice. Heat the neutral oil in a wok over medium heat. Add the pork, mushrooms, shrimp, scallion, and garlic. Add the five-spice powder, the soy sauce, the remaining 1 teaspoon cornstarch, and the toasted sesame oil and stir until the mixture forms a thick, saucy filling. Remove from the heat, transfer to a large bowl, cool, then refrigerate for 2 hours.

TO FINISH THE WRAPPERS AND SERVE:

PUT the wheat starch in a bowl and stir in the boiling (must be boiling!) water. Add the wheat starch mixture to the mashed taro, followed by the lard, baking soda, salt, and sugar. Knead the dough into a ball, then cut the dough into 24 equal-sized pieces.

TAKE one piece of dough, keeping the remaining dough covered with a damp cotton towel while you work, and create a small circular opening in the center with your thumb. Add 1 teaspoon of the chilled filling to the opening and press the filling into place inside the crevice so that you can fold the wrapper neatly around the sides. Pinch the dumpling closed, and with your hands, mold it into the shape of an egg.

REPEAT until all 24 dumplings are complete, then cover and put them into the refrigerator for at least 2 hours.

IN a large Dutch oven, heat 3 inches of oil to 375°F. Working in batches, deep-fry the dumplings for 2 to 3 minutes, until a nest-like texture appears on the surface of the dumplings. Carefully remove to a paper towel–lined plate to drain. Serve immediately.

THE TEA GURU: TIMOTHY HSU

Tim sat down in the chair in front of the shelf and asked me to sit on the other side. It was all very casual, but there was also something uplifting about how he did it. He set a small electric kettle to boil, and then he began carefully portioning out loose tea leaves from a tin behind him into a small silver sieve. This he placed in what looked like a small glass beaker. As the kettle clicked off, he poured the now-boiling water over the leaves, over which he placed a porcelain dome. After just a few moments, he lifted the dome and poured this tea into a small dark purple teapot with an intricate crosshatched design etched into its sides. Finally, he filled our cups—first mine, then his.

Though I literally grew up in a tea parlor, this was new to me, and I was intrigued by his deliberate movements. They were precise and graceful yet also seemed to flow naturally. We didn't talk business that evening or the next evening or the evening after that. Instead, as he poured delicate oolong and smoked cigars—his other main passion, it turns out—we connected on our passion for Chinatown, our desire to maintain the traditions that have sustained it, and our determination to keep this neighborhood and community we both loved so much thriving. Tim got me "tea drunk" that evening, as he has almost every time since. I stumbled out into the night of the Lower East Side absolutely buzzing. I couldn't sleep that evening, and when my wife asked me why, I told her the truth: I was thinking about tea.

Only later did I start buying tea from Tim for the Tea Parlor. It took a while both for me to fully appreciate what tea could contribute to the Nom Wah experience and, to be honest, for me to convince Tim that I was serious enough about it to be worthy of his precious teas. I've gotten tea drunk many times since then with Tim on some of the best teas in the world. But the simple, stately ceremony in his tea den never fails to fill me with awe.

I was born in 1973 and grew up in Hong Kong. I remember clearly how, when I was young, I would marvel at the small teapots that my father kept in the kitchen and from which he would pour tea for himself every afternoon. Our kitchen was filled with the delicate scent of my father's oolong tea, carried into the air by tendrils of steam. They floated into the air so slow and elegant compared the hectic pace of the rest of Hong Kong.

Because the teapots were so small, almost resembling dollhouse toys, they intrigued me. My father's collection seemed inexhaustible. The teapots came in infinite varieties, from whimsical animal shapes like fish and roosters to ones that were angular and modern. As my father explained, these small vessels were called yixing teapots. They had been made in the Wuxi region of Eastern China, in the Yangtze River valley, since at least the fifteenth century. They were prized by tea aficionados because, like cast-iron skillets,

after repeated use, the porous clay would retain the flavor of the tea brewed inside. The teapots, in other words, have memory.

As a child, I was forbidden from drinking the tea. I could get burned; I would definitely get hyper. But one day shortly after my twelfth birthday, my father invited me to sit with him and offered me my first cup of tea. I was proud to be asked to join him, but my initial impressions of the tea were not good. The liquid was bitter and astringent on my tongue. But I loved sitting with my father and the rest of my relatives as they spoke of "adult things," including little knowing asides to me, and slowly my appreciation for tea began to grow.

Hong Kong was, and still is, a frenetic city that makes New York feel like it's in slow motion. But my father served what is called *gongfu cha,* also known as *kung fu* tea. It is a traditional method of brewing and serving tea that originated in Chashan, in the eastern region of Guangdong, in the eighteenth century. The ceremony is less formal than a Japanese tea ceremony but based on the same principles: a mindfulness of the process, an appreciation of the fundamentals of steeping, the insight that it isn't the size of a cup of tea or the speed at which it is drunk that matters but rather the quality of the tea inside and the mind that esteems it.

Those minutes drinking tea seemed to slow time to a crawl, and in that space our family grew closer. Tea became inextricably linked to my experience of family. Soon I began collecting yixing teapots, chasing them down at Hong Kong's antique shops. When I moved to New York in 1990, I brought my collection of yixing pots with me.

I came to the States to study graphic design at the School of Visual Arts. Soon I landed a job as a graphic designer for a publishing house designing books. For years, my teapots were displayed in my loft in SoHo, but I seldom used them. In fact, I was so busy in the day-to-day of my career, I lost connection with many of my family's traditions. I rarely spoke Cantonese or even visited Chinatown.

Through a dear friend with strong family ties to the neighborhood, I became involved in the Charles B. Wang Center, which provides health care to many underserved Chinatown residents. As my connection with the Chinese American community grew deeper, my heart turned once again to tea. Especially with the older generations, sharing a cup of tea was the opening to a friendship. Tea is a handshake. When you say, "Let's have tea," they know that you want to talk. In fact, if you come to a place and you aren't offered tea, you'd better leave. You're not welcome. But it's more than just an expression of friendship. It's an expression of yourself. It is through how *I* perform the service and how *I* pour you tea that I can show a lot of who I am to you. I'm disarming myself and disarming you simultaneously.

Though I was still working in publishing and branding, I soon formed an informal tea club with a few other Chinatown tea aficionados. Once a month or so, we'd gather at one or the other of our houses, each proudly presenting the best teas we had found. There was no question that I had the most exquisite teapots, but when it came to the quality of the tea, mine was always inferior. Even when I had spent $100 on an ounce of tea, begging the tea merchants on Pell and Mott Streets for

with the Chong family to bring Canal Street Market to life. Canal Street Market is a food-and-crafts market in the crossroads of SoHo and Chinatown, on Canal between Broadway and Lafayette. Over the past twenty years, these blocks have been overrun with counterfeiters selling cheap knockoff goods and trinket shops with vast counterfeit wholesale operations in the back. After decades of decline along the once-vibrant western border of Chinatown, Canal Street Market is the first major commercial undertaking to revitalize the area. Through Philip Chong Jr. of Canal Street Market, I met Wilson.

Chinatown is a small community, and Nom Wah is an institution, so, of course, I knew of him. I had always admired how he approached the restaurant, with one foot in the door of tradition and the other in the future. I asked Wilson to tea and our relationship began.

Dim sum has always been linked to tea. Both dim sum and kung fu tea originate in the same region of southeastern China. What's more, much of dim sum evolved in the teahouses that lined the Silk Road. Like Chianti and cignale have in Tuscany, the two have coevolved. Tea, which is alkaline, both cuts the fat of traditional dim sum and mitigates the acidity that comes with spice and vinegar.

When I first started talking tea with Wilson, it was clear he didn't realize how much tea could add to the Nom Wah experience. But at least he was receptive. At Nom Wah, he served endless pots of bo-lay (more commonly known in Cantonese as pu'er tea), a perfectly acceptable and traditional accompaniment to dim sum.

their most premium leaves, it didn't compare to the leaves my fellow tea clubbers flashed during our get-togethers. I was learning the hard way: tea, like many things, is all about the human connection.

I was so obsessed that I began traveling back to Taiwan and mainland China—specifically, to the province of Fujian—to source teas myself. I traveled to the regions of Anxi and Yunnan and brought back delicate oolong and pu'er. In 2004, I opened the Mandarin's Tea Room, a private tearoom in SoHo, in order to bring other people into the world of kung fu tea. And even though I was still working in design, I also began to work

For years, as Nom Wah continued to become more and more popular, Wilson had been approached by dozens of tea companies, but we didn't start working together until 2017. He told me he wanted my tea, but I wasn't convinced. This isn't just my business; this is a passion, and I wanted to be sure that he understood the teas before I began a collaboration. After innumerable evenings sipping tea, I was convinced.

I wanted a special tea for Nom Wah that would be appropriate for both the food and the restaurant as a whole. I chose as the base a famous oolong tea from Anxi, an area of Eastern China in the Fujian province. The main city, Chaoshan, is a poor city itself, but what has given it its value for so many centuries is its port. All the things from the north, all the things from the south, all the things from the west, meet at Chaoshan. Like many port cities, it is chaotic, a jumble of new ideas and old traditions, of transients and of merchants. In this bustle, the Chaoshan learned to improvise, to collide old and new. When I walked into Nom Wah, I felt the same spirit of improvisation. Nom Wah is not traditional. Rather, it is traditional, but it's not a Chinese tradition Wilson is presenting. It's a Chinese American tradition, a mix of old and new.

Chaoshan teas are very respectful. They can abide all sorts of treatment and preparation and are pleasant partners for many flavors. Like everything else, the more care you give to the preparation of the tea, the more nuance you'll receive from it.

There are three premium teas on the menu at Nom Wah: T1, T2, and T3. T1 is the famous Anxi Tie Guanyin, or the Iron Goddess of Mercy. The tea is traditionally prepared with unroasted oolong harvested in spring, when the leaves are most flavorful. When infused correctly—not over- or underbrewed—you can almost taste fields of lilac and flourishes of sweet cream. Notes of vanilla and mandarin blossom weave in and out. The second tea, T2, is the same tea leaves but roasted. Though the floral sweetness shines through, it is given a garment of autumn fruit and roasted grains. A hearty tea, T2 can withstand several infusions without losing its subtlety. The third tea, T3, is the same as T1 with the addition of hand-harvested hydrangea leaves, which give it a subtle sweetness.

I know that in the high-volume reality of Nom Wah, it is unlikely my teas will be brewed and sipped with as much care as I would in my private tea den. There is no kung fu tea with its slow, deliberate movements or delicate slurping aeration. Nonetheless, I can see that those same sensations I had as a child, of connecting with another person over a cup of redolent steaming tea, happen every day, hundreds of times. The spirit of the tea lives.

ROLLS

CLOCKWISE FROM TOP LEFT: Shrimp Rice Rolls (p. 89); Plain Cheung Fun (p. 87); Vegetable Rice Rolls (p. 92); Cilantro and Scallion Rice Rolls (p. 89)

As crazy as it sounds, we're in the middle of a rice roll renaissance in New York. Cheung fun (腸粉), or Cantonese-style rice noodle rolls, are a popular treat in Guangdong. There, street food vendors set up steaming stalls on city streets where they churn out these silken delicacies, whose name literally means "intestine noodles," because they look like those glistening entrails. But, man, are they delicious. That's thousands of miles away from New York's Chinatown, yet for some reason, recently a handful of really fricking good cheung fun spots have cropped up near Nom Wah. There's Joe's Steam Rice Rolls at Canal Street Market, Hak Box across the Manhattan Bridge overpass from us, and Yi Ji Shi Mo Noodle Corp on Elizabeth Street to name a few.

It's been great for me, though I've gained ten pounds from rice rolls alone. There's no denying rice rolls are brilliant. The way traditional rice rolls are made (we make them slightly differently) involves grinding rice into a near-powder and using it to make a thickened slurry. This is then spread out thinly and steamed. It's almost like making a crepe. After a few minutes on a sheet pan in the steamer, the pale liquid slurry suddenly turns opaque and solid, creating a large rice noodle. Watching the vendor rolling the noodles up is as satisfying as sitting shotgun at the gas station and watching someone else clean the windshield. Ah, sweet squeegee ASMR.

Though Nom Wah is known for its dumplings, I have to say that of all the wrappers, this is my favorite. What I love about it is that the filling can go inside—as in shrimp and vegetable rolls—or into the actual liquid itself, as in cilantro scallion rolls. Don't sleep on cheung fun—they're supremely easy to make and even easier to eat, and though we don't list it here, you can most definitely throw some of your Master Fillings in here too if you're just a lonely wrapper looking for something to hold.

At the Tea Parlor, we use an industrial-sized big-ass hotel pan, but when making these at home, feel free to substitute in a 9½ x 13-inch quarter sheet pan. Basically, anything that allows you to form a thin layer will do.

CLOCKWISE FROM TOP CENTER:
Cilantro and Scallion Rice Rolls (p. 89);
Vegetable Rice Rolls (p. 92)

PLAIN CHEUNG FUN

MAKES 6 RICE ROLLS

1½ cups rice flour
3 tablespoons tapioca starch
1 tablespoon wheat starch
1 tablespoon potato starch
½ teaspoon salt
2½ cups lukewarm water
Neutral oil for greasing the pan

SIFT the rice flour, tapioca starch, wheat starch, potato starch, and salt into a large bowl. Mix in the lukewarm water, stirring until a consistency of very thin glue is reached.

WHEN ready to cook, mix again until there are no clumps. Using a brush, generously oil a rimmed quarter sheet pan. Using a ladle, pour just as much batter in the pan as needed to form a thin, even layer. (The thinner you can keep your roll, the better.)

SET up a steamer according to the instructions on page 10. Place the sheet pan in the steamer and steam for 6 minutes, or until you see bubbles on top of the mixture.

CAREFULLY remove the sheet pan from the steamer and set on a work surface (it will be hot, so be prudent). Let cool for a minute or so. Then, using a bench scraper, start rolling the rice roll from the top of the pan away from you until folded into a loose roll. Cut in half widthwise.

BRUSH the pan with oil again and repeat until you've used up all the batter.

WHEN ready to serve, briefly re-steam the rolls for 1 to 2 minutes until hot.

ROLLS

SWEET DIPPING SAUCE FOR CHEUNG FUN

½ cup light soy sauce
¾ cup dark soy sauce
¾ cup sugar
1 cup water
1½ teaspoons oyster sauce
1½ teaspoons chicken powder

HEAT a small saucepan to medium-low heat and add all ingredients. Stir until sugar and chicken powder are dissolved. Serve atop rice rolls.

SHRIMP RICE ROLLS AND CILANTRO AND SCALLION RICE ROLLS

ice rolls can be filled either before or after they are steamed. If you're placing the filling in the pre-steamed roll, you effectively use the same steam to cook the roll as you do what's inside it. Cool, right? Shrimp rolls are like that. Ditto cilantro and scallion rolls. In both the slightly sweet but mostly textural wrapper of the rice roll is the canvas for the sweetness of the shrimp, in one case, and the herbaceous nature of the greens, in the other. Though the recipe is for cilantro and scallion, feel free to experiment with other herbs of your choosing.

SHRIMP RICE ROLLS

MAKES ABOUT 6 ROLLS

1 recipe Plain Cheung Fun (page 87)
18 medium shrimp, peeled, deveined, and patted dry

MAKE the batter for the rice rolls. After you pour the rice slurry into your pan, put 6 shrimp onto each roll, placing them 1 inch from the edges. Steam as directed and serve immediately.

CILANTRO AND SCALLION RICE ROLLS

MAKES ABOUT 6 ROLLS

2 tablespoons finely chopped fresh cilantro
2 tablespoons finely chopped scallion
1 recipe Plain Cheung Fun (page 87)

IN a small bowl, mix the cilantro and scallion. **MAKE** the batter for the rice rolls. After you pour the rice slurry into your pan, sprinkle the herbs on top, dividing them evenly. Steam as directed and serve immediately.

YOUTIAO (FRIED DOUGH)

Some rice noodle rolls are filled post facto. In these cases the fillings are distinct, more akin to the burrito paradigm. Youtiao, Chinese savory churro, are a good example of this. Youtiao is the ultimate breakfast food—an indicator of dim sum's origins as matutinal fare—and is often dipped in congee (rice porridge). It's our equivalent of a croissant in a latte. When youtiao is wrapped in cheung fun it is called *ja leung*, a glorious if all too rare instance of carb-on-carb in the Cantonese kitchen. You can make youtiao from scratch, but it's a hassle. We buy ours from Twin Marquis on Canal Street in Chinatown in New York, but you can also buy them online, in internet Chinatown. Though they come already cooked, we deep-fry them for extra crunch.

1 cup neutral oil
3 youtiao
1 recipe Plain Cheung Fun (page 87)

IN a deep pot or wok, heat the neutral oil to 375°F. Add the youtiao and fry for 5 minutes, or until golden brown. Remove, and place on paper towel–lined plate to drain. Pat dry.
AFTER rice rolls are steamed, enclose 1 youtiao in each as you roll them.

VEGETABLE RICE ROLLS

MAKES ABOUT 6 ROLLS

Unlike dumplings, one doesn't actually *cook* the filling of cheung fun in the cheung fun itself. So I wouldn't recommend using Pork Master Filling or Shrimp Master Filling here. You can, however, use No Pork No Shrimp Master Filling, since the vegetables have been precooked. Just be careful when you fill the rolls because the filling doesn't cling together naturally.

1 recipe Plain Cheung Fun (page 87)
1 recipe No Pork No Shrimp Master Filling (page 43)

AFTER your rice rolls are fully steamed, line 3 tablespoons of filling ½ inch from the edges. **FOLD** the lip over, then complete the folding.

STEAMED SPARERIB RICE ROLLS

MAKES ABOUT 6 ROLLS

You can also make cheung fun with steamed spareribs. This is a classic dim sum item, frequently ordered by the old-timers at Nom Wah. To me it doesn't make sense, because the silkiness of the rice roll is offset by the crunchy cartilage of the steamed spareribs on which many like to chew. However, from what I observe, people like to alternate bites of noodle and steamed sparerib. Silky and crunchy, a classic combo.

Evenly spreading the spareribs along the edge of each steamed rice noodle a quarter inch from the edge allows you the ability to execute one fold before you reach the meat. Then roll up like a body in a carpet. You know what I'm talking about.

1 recipe Plain Cheung Fun (page 87)
12 ounces Steamed Spareribs (page 180)

AFTER your rice rolls are fully steamed, enclose 2 ounces or so of spareribs in each as you roll.

BEAN CURD ROLLS

MAKES 12 ROLLS

I continue to stand in awe of the versatility of the soybean. Soy products hold a place of pride in Chinese cuisine, from tofu (also known as bean curd) to liquified, fermented soybeans in the form of soy sauce. In the realm of dim sum, where everything becomes either wrapping or filling, soybean finds itself on both sides of the divide. Here it lives as bean curd skin, a wrapper. Bean curd skin is formed by boiling soy milk, which forms a solid layer on top of the liquid. This is then dried and sold. Since there is no coagulant, it isn't technically tofu, but who cares? It combines tofu's delicate flavor with the ability to wrap itself around an array of fillings. Unlike dumplings, these bean curd rolls must be fried first and *then* steamed. I suppose you could make your own tofu skin, but we buy Dragon bean curd skin, which has six sheets per package. Just be extremely careful handling the package, as—just like people's skin—dry bean curd skin cracks.

1 tablespoon cornstarch
2½ tablespoons water
5 sheets dried bean curd skin
1 recipe Pork Master Filling (page 41)
¼ cup bamboo shoots, julienned
3 tablespoons neutral oil
2 scallions, diced, for garnish
Oyster sauce for serving

IN a small bowl, mix the cornstarch with the water to form a paste (this will be the glue that holds the edges of the bean curd skin together).

CAREFULLY remove the dried bean curd skin sheets from the package. Soak each sheet separately in warm water for a minute or so to make it pliable. When ready to stuff one, carefully transfer it to a paper towel.

CUT the tofu skin diagonally. Place 3 tablespoons of the Pork Master Filling on the long edge of the triangle. Equally divide the bamboo shoots among the skins atop the filling. No need to leave a buffer.

ROLL the skin over once, then fold in the corners and roll again like a joint.

USE the cornstarch paste to moisten the edges and seal the skin together.

HEAT the neutral oil in a large nonstick pan over medium-high heat. Pan-fry the rolls, in batches if needed, flipping constantly but taking care not to allow them to open, for approximately 5 minutes, until golden. Remove with a spider or tongs onto a paper towel–lined plate to drain.

TOP: Steamed Shrimp Bean Curd Skin Rolls (p. 95);
BOTTOM: Bean Curd Rolls (p. 93)

SET up a steamer according to the instructions on page 10. Steam the roll, in batches if needed, for about 8 minutes until bean curd is silken. Remove from the steamer, top with the scallions, and serve immediately, with oyster sauce on the side.

VARIATION:
STEAMED SHRIMP BEAN CURD SKIN ROLLS

For a healthier alternative—but a no less delicious one—sub out the Pork Master Filling for Shrimp Master Filling (page 42) and throw in about ¼ cup of finely chopped scallions for extra crunch.

VARIATION:
VEGETABLE BEAN CURD SKIN ROLLS

What if I told you that you could sub out the Pork Master Filling for No Pork No Shrimp Master Filling (page 43) in the same quantity? Would you be stoked? Would you be surprised? Would you be like, "Finally, a vegan option in a dim sum book! It's about goddamn time!"?

OPTIONAL:
CHINESE GRAVY FOR STEAMED BEAN CURD ROLLS

Instead of the oyster sauce, you can serve this gravy over your steamed bean curd rolls. This recipe makes enough for one batch of rice rolls.

¾ teaspoon kosher salt
½ teaspoon sugar
¼ teaspoon MSG
¾ teaspoon oyster sauce
¼ teaspoon ground white pepper
½ teaspoon toasted sesame oil
½ teaspoon dark soy sauce (you can add more for deeper color)
¾ cup water
1 tablespoon potato starch

IN a small saucepan, whisk together all the ingredients except the potato starch over medium heat until the sauce comes to a simmer. Add the potato starch, whisking until dissolved completely. When it comes to a boil, remove the pan from the heat. Immediately pour over your steamed bean curd rolls.

SPRING ROLLS

MAKES 10 ROLLS

Though they are technically rolls, I always think of spring rolls (春卷) more as cigar-shaped dumplings since the filling is so dependent on the wrapper. Though spring rolls are high up in the empyrean of Chinese American food, they're often freebies, Asian lagniappe that come with the Special #5 Combo. And despite the fact that they're meant to be filled with fresh vegetables and were traditionally eaten during the spring festival—when the earth came alive with the bounty of healthy living!—they have a bad reputation as grease-leaden bloat sticks. But that's not the fault of the roll but of slapdash frying. At their best, spring rolls are bright and crunchy with a fresh vegetable payload, both virtuous and toothsome. Just make sure your oil is hot enough so when you fry the rolls, they don't become oil-logged.

1 tablespoon cornstarch
2½ tablespoons water
10 sheets square spring roll wrappers
1 recipe No Pork No Shrimp Master Filling (page 43)
Neutral oil
2 scallions, diced, for garnish
Oyster sauce for serving

IN a small bowl, mix the cornstarch with the water to create your sealing slurry.

PLACE a wrapper on a clean, dry surface, with a corner we'll call South facing you. Add about 3 tablespoons of filling in a cigar shape from the East corner to the West corner, leaving about 2 inches of clearance from each corner of the wrapper.

FOLD in the East and West corners to slightly overlap atop the filling. Then fold up the South corner toward the North, covering the filling. Roll once more.

APPLY the cornstarch mixture to exposed edges of the wrapper. Fold over to close.

IN a large saucepan, heat 3 inches of neutral oil over medium-high to 350°F.

WORKING in two batches, fry the rolls until lightly browned and crisp, turning as needed, 3 to 5 minutes. Transfer to paper towels to drain.

SERVE immediately topped with scallions and oyster sauce on the side.

MAKE AHEAD: You can assemble the spring rolls ahead of time and freeze them unfried. When ready to fry, do so straight from frozen—do not thaw.

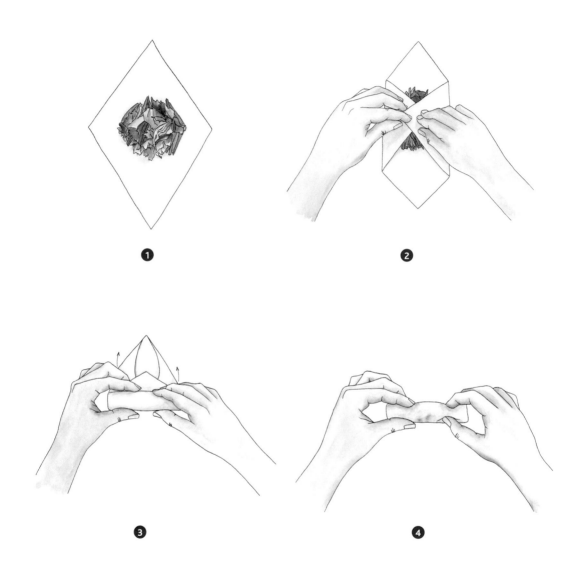

1

2

3

4

OG EGG ROLLS

MAKES 6 EGG ROLLS

Let's just admit it: the egg roll has a terrible reputation. It's the wallflower of the Chinese American menu. But that's only because so few restaurants take the time to actually make a proper version. Crack open a normcore egg roll and good luck finding eggs anywhere in the thing. The wrapper is wheat; the filling is cabbage. The eggs are phantoms. But at Nom Wah, we make legit egg rolls—OG egg rolls, as we call them—made like they should be, with actual eggs.

The egg roll is a true son of the Chinese American kitchen. In fact, according to Andrew Coe, author of *Chop Suey*, the egg roll was invented a few blocks away from Nom Wah in the early twentieth century at Lung Fong on Canal Street, one of the pioneering Chinese American banquet restaurants in New York. But it couldn't have been much later that Nom Wah started making one.

When I took over the Tea Parlor, one of the items my Uncle Wally was most proud of—in fact, one of the only items Uncle Wally was proud of—was the egg roll. The reason is simple: we take the time and make the effort to give an egg roll the respect it deserves. Every morning, a chef comes into the kitchen, heats up a 9-inch pan, and starts to make delicate egg crepes. Silky and impossibly thin, the hundreds he makes form a tower that resembles a *mille crêpe* cake but . . . eggier.

Today, when an order comes in, we hand-fold the egg roll, wrapping it around a vegetable filling. Then we coat the package in a mixture of flour and water and fry in hot oil until golden. The result is a crispy, flavorful baton that breaks open to reveal the delicate flavor and texture of the crepe and the succulent filling. When I watch a new customer break open the egg roll, I love to see their face light up. It's got the surprise of something you thought you knew but didn't, like in those scenes in high school rom-coms, when the nerd comes back after summer as the coolest kid on campus, and all the kids in the hallway are like, "Oh, damn. What did I miss?"

6 ounces boneless, skinless chicken breast
2 tablespoons neutral oil, plus more for brushing and frying
10 large eggs, beaten
2 tablespoons light soy sauce
2 tablespoons cornstarch
1 tablespoon Shaoxing wine
1 teaspoon toasted sesame oil
1¼ teaspoons sugar
10 dried shiitake mushrooms
½ cup bamboo shoots, julienned
½ cup whole small button mushrooms (halved if larger)
½ cup chopped baby corn
½ cup finely chopped celery
½ cup chopped water chestnuts
1 small carrot, julienned
1 clove garlic, minced
Kosher salt
Ground white pepper
1 cup plus 1 tablespoon water
1 cup all-purpose flour

PREHEAT the oven to 350°F.

PLACE the chicken on baking sheet, transfer to the oven, and cook through, approximately 40 minutes. Let cool briefly, then, using a fork, shred the meat. Set aside.

MEANWHILE, heat a 9-inch nonstick skillet over medium-high heat. Brush the skillet lightly with neutral oil, then add ⅙ of the beaten eggs, swirling the pan to coat evenly. Cook until lightly browned on the bottom and just set, 1 to 2 minutes. Transfer the egg crepe to a plate and cover loosely to keep warm. Repeat until finished.

IN a small bowl, whisk the soy sauce with 1 tablespoon of the cornstarch, the wine, the toasted sesame oil, and ¼ teaspoon of the sugar.

SUBMERGE mushrooms in hot water for 20 to 30 minutes until tender. Remove, drain, and dice.

IN a wok or large skillet, heat the 2 tablespoons neutral oil until shimmering. Add the shiitakes, bamboo shoots, button mushrooms, baby corn, celery, water chestnuts, carrot, and garlic. Stir-fry over medium-high heat until the vegetables are softened, about 8 minutes. Add the soy sauce mixture and cook until thickened, about 2 minutes.

SCRAPE into a bowl, stir in the shredded chicken, and season with salt and white pepper. Let cool completely, then refrigerate until chilled, about 30 minutes.

IN a small bowl, whisk 1 tablespoon cornstarch with 1 tablespoonwater.

TO assemble, follow the folding instructions for the Spring Rolls (page 98).

OVER medium-high heat, in a large saucepan, bring 3 inches of vegetable oil to 350°F.

IN a medium bowl, whisk the flour and the remaining 1 teaspoon sugar. Whisk in the remaining 1 cup water until smooth.

DIP 3 of the egg rolls in the flour batter. Using tongs, carefully lower the egg rolls into the hot oil. Fry until lightly browned and crisp, turning as needed to ensure they are evenly colored, 3 to 5 minutes. Transfer to paper towels to drain. Repeat the coating and frying process with the remaining egg rolls. Serve immediately.

THE FISH WHISPERER: FREEMAN WONG OF AQUA BEST SEAFOOD

When I was growing up, my parents never took me to the New York Aquarium to marvel at the tropical fish darting through the water, the stingrays gliding as if in flight, and the piranhas looking murderously through the plate glass. They didn't need to. We had Grand Street between Bowery and Allen, where the sidewalks were crowded with seafood stalls, each packed to the gills with an endless array of fish. Gray sole gazed up at me, unseeing, from their Styrofoam boxes, as I gazed at them, eyes wide with wonder. Monkfish, ugly puddle of a sea creature—later I learned they are delicious too—were permanently frowning, contemplating their cruel fate. In aquarium tanks, lobsters with their claws banded shut pedaled their legs futilely. Carp swam so close to one another in their purgatory they looked like commuters on the A train at rush hour. There were barrels full of crabs morosely moving atop one another and a tangle of crawfish, angry and peevish. Around them, men in rubber boots with white jackets held hoses to wash down their goods. The water running from the tile floor out onto the street sometimes ran red. This was a striking scene for a young boy, an onslaught of odors and sights and thorny moral questions.

But there was hardly any time to ponder the existential issues. These stores were crowded, chaotic marketplaces with narrow aisles that were crowded with blue-collar Chinese shoppers, plastic bags in tow and frequently in raucous discussion over which fish exactly they wanted. "Give me the one with shiny eyes!" "Not that one! It's too small!" "Not that one, too big!" "Do you take me for a fool?" Once the unlucky fish had been identified, the fishmonger would dip his net into the tank, extract the shimmering, wriggling fish, and pound its head with a wooden club that reminded me of a baseball bat until it stilled.

As a Chinese American, this was at the outer fringes of my comfort zone. For many Chinese, the matter-of-fact killing is the necessary step that takes place before a fish becomes dinner. But for Americans, to see the transition from life to death—though we're grateful it happens—is a shock.

Now, when I walk down Grand Street with my kids, their eyes widen in similar wonder as we pass the fishmongers. Many, of course, have been replaced by art galleries and coffee shops with shiny espresso machines. After the Fulton Fish Market moved up to the Bronx, the bustle of the Chinatown seafood world stilled a bit. That, along with the slow gentrification of the area, has driven many fishmongers either out of business or to the outer boroughs. But there are still places that instill in me, and now in Lucy and Ryan, that same awe.

One of those places is Aqua Best Seafood. On any given day, the glass doors of the store are wide

open. Inside a box, crimson crayfish scrum. In tanks lining one wall, horseshoe crabs—some upturned, some upright—scramble to no avail. Eels wriggle. Monkfish, still ugly, shine. From their funereal ice beds, catfish and branzino are displayed. The fish here have red gills, glassy eyes, and flesh that bounces back. They are unsurpassingly fresh. And there's Freeman Wong, standing behind the cash register, always wearing a fleece vest, always with his phone out fielding calls from chefs, always with a smile.

He, his brother Stephen, their formidable mother, and a gray tabby cat named Mimi the Bodega Cat run the place. Freeman and I first met in 2016, when I began buying his product for Fung Tu, my short-lived modern Chinese American expansion on the Lower East Side. After Fung Tu closed in 2017, Freeman and I remained friends. Since then I've returned to Aqua Best hundreds of times with my family, by myself, for fun, for work. And I always wanted to know how Freeman got where he was and where he wanted to go.

I grew up in the shadow of this business. My father founded Aqua Best back in the late '70s shortly after he arrived from Hong Kong. Like many immigrant families, our journey wasn't a one-way street. My grandfather Duo Deng was the first Wong to emigrate, arriving from Fujian province, by way of Hong Kong, in Philadelphia in the 1960s. He left his son (my father), his brother, his two sisters, and his wife behind. Like so many immigrants, he found work in the restaurants of Philly's Chinatown. (Philadelphia had, and has, a Chinatown that rivals New York. Almost.) My grandfather was a hard worker and smart too. When one of the restaurant owners offered to sponsor him, he asked instead that the man sponsor my father, Frankie Wong. My dad was in his twenties, already married with two children, although I was not yet born.

Like his father, my dad found work in Philadelphia's restaurants, but he soon moved to New York with big plans. With the help of my mother, he founded a small vegetable stand on Catherine Street and serviced the local community. Gradually he expanded to include a butcher shop, a grocery store, and a fish market, all on the Lower East Side. My father partnered with his extended family, so at one point, many of the stores on that block of Catherine Street were owned by us or our cousins.

I was born around this time, 1976, at the full flower of my father's ventures. My family lived in a small apartment on Clinton Street, but I didn't stay there long. Shortly after I was born, we took a family vacation to Hong Kong. My sister, my older brother, my father, and my mother returned to New York—but they left me behind. For four years, I lived with my maternal grandmother, seeing my family only when they visited Hong Kong. I remember little about this time, except vague memories of sitting on the patio of my grandmother's apartment, overlooking a valley full of houses and rooftops.

Eventually, around 1982, my parents fetched me. When I returned, I enrolled in kindergarten at St. Joseph's, a Catholic school on the Lower East Side. My dad was busy traveling up and down the Eastern Seaboard building relationships with the

STONE CRAB $2.99 Lb

fishermen who fished conch in Virginia or fluke in the Long Island Sound or whiting in New Jersey. It was his insight that in order to compete with the Fulton Fish Market, a few blocks away, he needed to go straight to the source. My siblings and I stayed behind with my mom and were ferried to Chinese school and music lessons, hung out (and helped) at the shop, and played stickball in East River Park. It was a pretty carefree existence.

Everything changed on the night of November 3, 1987, when my father and two of his friends were murdered. The shop our family ran at that time was on 81 Catherine Street, between Monroe and Cherry Streets. It was right around the corner from where we lived. That night, it was getting late and my dad hadn't come home. My mom went down to the shop to check in on him and found my father

and two of his friends who used to hang around at the shop dead. I was eleven at the time, and my brother was eight, so the rest of the family made sure that we two didn't find out any details. To the best of my knowledge, the crime was never solved.

As soon as my father died, the entire family mobilized around the business. My mother, who had always been peripherally involved, took the reins. She is a strong, shrewd woman. Whereas my father basically sold to other fish markets, my mother wanted to expand from wholesale to processing and eventually retail. That was a whole lot of work, and my siblings and I soon joined too. Suddenly our nights, weekends, and after-school hours were occupied by the shop. Our fate was left to ourselves.

On weekends, we'd pile into the cab of a box truck and drive out to Long Island or up to Massachusetts or down to Virginia in search of local conch. (Italians call it *scungilli;* Chinese call it 海螺 or *hoi lo*). We'd return to New York, smash the shells, extract the meat, and then freeze it. The business grew from supplying a few fish markets in the city to a brisk operation selling our seafood to Hong Kong and other parts of Asia. When I was in high school, I'd spend the summers in Martha's Vineyard at our buying station. I'd wake up in the early morning to help the fishermen chop up the horseshoe crabs they used as bait. At night, when they returned, I'd pick up the conch and comb through and sort them. Only then would they be trucked down to New York and processed.

There were a few Chinese Americans on the island at the time. Most of them were in the

restaurant business. We were one of the few doing seafood. It was terribly hard work, but I still relished the clean air and a rare chance to get away from the hustle and bustle of city life.

By the time I graduated from college, I was fully immersed in the business. Having one foot in America and the other in China allowed me and my younger brother, Stephen, to better serve and expand our customer base beyond just our Chinese clients. One of the first things we realized was how much Americans hate seeing their fish alive. For us Chinese, the ability to pick our own dinner while it is still swimming proves its freshness. Americans, on the hand, prefer their fish to appear, as if by magic, already filleted. For that reason, we find non-Chinese customers like bigger fish like wild striped bass and halibut, cut into smaller pieces, whereas Chinese prefer one- to two-pound fish like tilapia or gray sole with a silky flesh that turns pearlescent when steamed.

Just like my mom did before us, we're constantly innovating. My brother struck a friendship with Dorothy Cann Hamilton, the late dean of the nearby French Culinary Institute.

Dorothy had grown up in Cape Breton, Nova Scotia, the granddaughter of a fisherman, and had fond memories of a lobster there called the Fourchu lobster, named after the village off which it is caught. At the time these were nearly impossible to get in New York, and really anywhere in the United States, but through Dorothy, we developed a relationship with the Nova Scotian fishermen up there. The lobsters, which develop a sweeter flavor thanks to the cold water, are available for only ten weeks every year. The competition is fierce when they arrive.

Our latest venture is Essex Pearl, a forty-seat sit-down restaurant in the basement food hall of a fancy building in the Lower East Side. Why, we wondered, are we only selling our fish and seafood to other chefs when we could be showcasing it with a restaurant of our own? At our new place, we're be able to feature types of seafood that are often overlooked, such as scorpion fish from Dominica, among others. We showcase all of our hard work, the decades spent building relationships with fishermen here and in Canada, on the plate. Instead of simply selling our lobsters to another chef, we prepare them with black bean brown butter, clementine, and edamame, and serve it ourselves.

When I look back over the journey of our business from my father to my mother and now to me and my brother, I'm sure my father would be proud of where the business is today, even if he might not recognize it.

I am now the father of three teenagers, the youngest of whom is about the age I was when I lost my father. We live on the Lower East Side, just blocks from where I grew up. Thankfully, my brother Stephen, who does not yet have kids, does most of the travel for the business, so I can drive my kids to school every day. Something that my family has taught me—both professionally and personally—is that building connections and being present are the most important things you can do.

CAKES

We call them cakes and yet they are not truly cakes. One is a pancake; the others, though loaf-like, are neither bready nor baked. But cakes are my favorite section of the dim sum menu. Turnip cakes (lo bak go)—which are actually made with Chinese radish (daikon), not turnip—are a staple in all dim sum houses. Studded with Chinese sausage, dried shrimp, and mushrooms, lo bak go combine the unique, slightly sweet flavor of the daikon with a grab bag of fillings. Every bite is a jackpot. When sliced and pan-fried, lo bak go is a study in contrasts, featuring a crispy crust and a tender interior. Like everything else, it seems, turnip cakes were traditionally eaten during Chinese New Year—because the word for radish kinda sounds like the word for good fortune. Thankfully, we now have the good fortune of eating radish year-round. Please note that you'll need to plan ahead when making lo bak go because it has to chill overnight to set.

SCALLION PANCAKES

MAKES 8 PANCAKES

Every country has its crepe, and the scallion pancake (葱油饼 or cung you bing) is ours. While Western pancakes are made with batter, this one is made with many layers of flaky dough studded with scallions. They're crisp and delicious snacks, as popular as a breakfast for school kids as a late-night snack for drunken revelers. (Ever consider how much drunk food and kid food overlap?) When I look around Nom Wah, I'll often see every single table with an order of scallion pancakes, and I laugh. If only they knew how easy these are to make, we'd be out of business.

3 cups all-purpose flour, plus more for kneading
1⅓ cups boiling water
4 teaspoons toasted sesame oil
8 scallions, chopped
1 teaspoon salt
½ cup neutral oil
Dumpling Dipping Sauce (page 35) for serving

PLACE the flour in a large bowl. Add the boiling water and stir with a wooden spoon until the dough forms a ball.

TURN the dough out onto a floured surface and knead until smooth and elastic, 4 to 6 minutes. The dough should not be sticky to the touch, nor should it stick to the table. Place in a large bowl, cover, and let rest for 30 minutes.

ONCE rested, divide the dough into 8 equal-sized pieces. Roll each piece into a thin circle, 8 inches in diameter. Brush each circle with ½ teaspoon toasted sesame oil and evenly sprinkle with 1 heaping tablespoon of scallion and ⅛ teaspoon salt. Starting with the side closest to you, roll the disc well, like you would a joint. Then, working from one side, roll into a coil. Finally, use your rolling pin to evenly flatten the coil to ⅛-inch thickness.

IN a large skillet, heat 1 tablespoon of the neutral oil over medium-high heat. Cook the pancakes one at a time, adding another tablespoon of oil for each pancake, until golden brown, 2 to 3 minutes on each side. Serve immediately, with dipping sauce if desired.

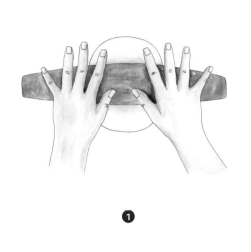

1

2

3

4

5

TURNIP CAKES

SERVES 6

5 dried shiitake mushrooms
2 medium daikon (Chinese radishes), approximately 2½ pounds
½ teaspoon kosher salt
3 tablespoon neutral oil, plus more for greasing
1 link Chinese sausage, roughly chopped
1 tablespoon dried shrimp, soaked in warm water for 30 minutes, dried, then roughly chopped
½ teaspoon sugar
½ teaspoon chicken powder
1¼ cups rice flour
Ground white pepper
1 tablespoon cornstarch
1 scallion, finely chopped
Hoisin sauce for serving

SUBMERGE mushrooms in hot water for 20 to 30 minutes until tender. Drain and roughly chop.

PEEL the daikon and grate it on the largest holes of a box grater. Transfer to a large bowl along with the salt and mix together lightly. Cover with plastic wrap and let sit for 20 minutes.

WRAP the daikon in a kitchen towel and squeeze it over a bowl. Set the dry daikon aside. If you have less than 3⅓ cups of daikon water in the bowl, add enough warm tap water to reach that amount.

IN a large pot, preferably with a wide bottom, heat 1 tablespoon of the neutral oil over medium heat. Add the sausage, along with the hydrated shrimp and mushrooms, and cook, stirring constantly, until you see fat releasing from the sausage and it becomes slightly crisp, approximately 2 minutes.

USING a slotted spoon, transfer the sausage, shrimp, and mushrooms to a small bowl. Leave the fat in the pot. Stir in the dry daikon, sugar, and chicken powder. Cook, stirring constantly, for 2 minutes. Do not brown. Add the daikon water and bring to a boil, stirring frequently, then lower the heat to medium-low.

IN a small bowl, whisk the rice flour, white pepper, and cornstarch, then whisk in just as much water as needed to form a slurry. Add the slurry to the pot and stir constantly for 2 minutes, or until a thick paste has formed. Turn off the heat. Return the sausage, shrimp, and mushrooms to the pot and stir to combine.

STEAM according to instructions on page 10. Oil a 9 x 13-inch baking dish, and use a rubber spatula to distribute the mixture evenly into the dish. Place the dish in the steamer and steam for 45 minutes to 1 hour, until cake is pearlescent and holds its form. Let cool in the refrigerator overnight.

TO portion, remove the turnip cake from the baking dish, either by cutting it into pieces

and removing with a spatula or, preferably, turning it out whole. If the latter, cut in half, then lengthwise in thirds, again lengthwise in thirds, and then across in thirds to form flat squares.

HEAT the remaining 2 tablespoons neutral oil a large nonstick skillet over medium heat. Place the turnip cake slices in the pan,

working in batches if needed. Cook, without stirring or moving them, for 3 to 4 minutes, until the turnip cakes are crispy on one side. Flip and repeat on the other side. Transfer to a paper towel–lined plate to drain excess oil.

TO serve, place the slices on a serving platter, garnish with the scallion, and serve with hoisin sauce.

TARO HASH CAKES

MAKES 12 CAKES

When we first opened Nom Wah Nolita in 2016 with Calvin Eng, I was impressed by the reckless abandon with which he mashed together the dim sum we'd been making for nearly a century—which comes from a tradition thousands of years old—with foods from the more recent past. This, for instance, is the marriage between a classic Jewish nosh of the Lower East Side and a classic Chinese ingredient. I would wager that the Chinese root vegetable taro was unknown in the shtetls of Europe. But Calvin loved latkes, those fried potato pancakes eaten at Hanukkah, and he resolved to Nom Wah–ify them. Here the taro is the body double for the potato, the plum sauce is the applesauce, and the labneh—the first and only time labneh made a cameo at Nom Wah—stands in for the sour cream.

FOR THE CAKES:
2 pounds taro root, cleaned, peeled, and quartered lengthwise
1 large yellow onion
1 tablespoon salt
2 teaspoons ground black pepper
1 tablespoon garlic powder
1 tablespoon cornstarch
Neutral oil for frying

FOR THE GARNISHES:
2 tablespoons plum sauce
2 tablespoons labneh
1 bunch scallions, sliced
Trout roe (if you're fancy)

PUT the taro into a pot of cold water, cover, and bring to a boil over high heat. Boil until just pierceable with a fork, 5 to 8 minutes after the water starts to boil (keep a close eye, as taro tends to go from rock-hard to mushy in seconds).

MEANWHILE, roughly grate the yellow onion. Place it inside a dish towel and wring it out over the sink to remove all of the water.

ONCE fork-tender (but not mushy), drain, pat the taro dry, and roughly grate. Put in a large bowl along with the grated onion, salt, black pepper, garlic power, and cornstarch.

FORM cakes the size of a hockey puck (about 3 ounces), using a scale or a large ice cream scoop to measure and your hands to shape them.

ADD enough oil to a large cast-iron skillet to reach 1 inch in depth. Heat over medium heat, then add your taro cakes, working in batches if necessary. Pan-fry on both sides until golden brown and crispy, approximately 5 to 7 minutes, pressing down gently every so often to create a good sear.

SERVE with garnishes of your choice.

THE QUEEN OF PEARL RIVER:
JOANNE KWONG OF PEARL RIVER MART

Because I'm tall, everyone thinks I played basketball growing up. No, like every other Chinese kid, I did karate. Kung fu, actually, at a place called Yee's Hung Ga on Henry Street. I wasn't very good at it, and—between Chinese school, Kaplan tutoring, and working at my dad's supermarket—my interest in the martial arts fizzled. By far, the best part of my early kung fu career was when it was time to buy a new pair of black cotton-soled kung fu shoes. Because that meant a trip to Pearl River Mart.

For anyone who hasn't been, first of all, go. Brace yourself for a cacophony of colors and clothing and vases and incense and tchotchkes and snacks and umbrellas and slippers and dragons and weird beauty products—I don't know what they do. Pearl River feels like an ancient bazaar crossed with a Duane Reade and a Toys"R"Us. (Toys"R"Us used to be a toy store, for you kids.) But there's truly nowhere else in the world like Pearl River Mart. Pearl River, as everyone calls it, was the world's first Chinese American department store when it opened in 1971 and, like any department store, it pretty much stocked anything anyone could ever need. As a kid, I ignored the boring stuff like vacuum cleaners and plates and geeked out on the elaborately embroidered cheongsam dresses, the small boxes of sandalwood incense, the nunchakus and tsais, and, of course, shoes.

Even though I quit kung fu before reaching absolute mastery, over the years I'd find myself back at Pearl River, buying everything from a mop to stickers to plates for my home. And though it moved from one location to another, remarkably, pushing open the doors and walking in felt exactly the same: like entering into the mind of your zany hoarder aunt from the mainland.

Like every other New Yorker, when word broke that Pearl River had lost its lease and was closing up shop in 2015, I was fucking bummed. Pearl River is like a polar ice cap. You think it's always going to be there, but what you don't realize is that slowly it's been receding until—boom!—it's too late. It's gone and we're all gonna die. So, again, like every other New Yorker, when news broke that Joanne Kwong, the wife of the owner's son, was stepping in to rescue Pearl River from destruction, I was overjoyed. Kung fu shoes forever!

Over the last five years, as I've gotten to know Joanne, my admiration for her has only grown. We see eye-to-eye on so many issues facing multigenerational businesses in Chinatown, and I've admired how she's navigated safeguarding all that Pearl River was while exploring what it can be. Whenever I'd see Joanne at Chinatown functions, we never seemed to have enough time for our

conversations, so I was happy for the chance to sit with her for a rare quiet moment to discuss her life and the life of Pearl River.

My mother-in-law seemed defeated. It was Thanksgiving 2015 and we were all gathered around the table. My husband, Gene, and I, our sons, Milo and Griffin, my mom, my sister with her husband and daughters, my sister-in-law Michelle, and my in-laws, Mr. and Mrs. Chen.

The Chens' store, Pearl River Mart, one of the few Asian American department stores in the country, was world famous. An iconic destination. But now, like many small businesses in New York, it seemed to be on its last legs. The lease for its sprawling three-story location in SoHo was ending that year, and the landlord told my in-laws he intended to increase the rent fivefold, from $1 million to $6 million per year. (Yes, you read that right.) Staying at that rate was out of the question, so for about a year, we kids had tried to help the Chens figure out their options.

As second-generation immigrant kids, my husband, sisters-in-law, and I had all attended good schools and built stable careers. We tried to help in the way that we knew how: by activating our networks to get to the right answers. We dragged Mom and Dad to meet friends of friends who could offer advice as investment bankers, retail consultants, small business experts, and various and sundry potential buyers, investors, and partners.

In typical expedient fashion, they entertained these meetings for a short time, then were done, hoping to find the right successor but also satisfied if necessary to exit, as they put it, "nobly." My in-laws are two of the most principled, humble, elegant people I know, and as a rule, they don't linger or dwell in the past. They felt they had accomplished their original mission. If it was their time to go, they reasoned, they would do so with pride and dignity intact. In the beginning, they would tell us of a promising option here, an interested buyer there—lots of people were distraught at the idea of an NYC without Pearl River—and we would ask how those possibilities were going. But nothing was quite right. Most wanted to strip the business apart, use the name, and make as much money as possible. For the Chens, money had always been beside the point.

My mother-in-law sighed and looked incredibly tired. In the more than twenty years I had known her, I had never seen her, or my father-in-law, anything less than exuberantly cheerful and hopeful, always hopeful. Perhaps it was indeed time to close up, she said. After nearly half a century, the facts were undeniable: the retail landscape was changing, commercial rent in NYC was becoming untenable, and the business simply could not continue without a new leader full of energy and fresh ideas. She was silent for a moment, and then uttered the two words that changed my life: "Anyone interested?"

IN 1971, MY FATHER-IN-LAW, MING YI CHEN, was something of a radical leader in Manhattan's Chinatown. He had immigrated to the United States from Taiwan in the late 1960s. Immigration laws had changed in 1965, allowing in more non-Europeans, and along with the Chens came a wave of the best and brightest students and skilled workers from all over the world. Mr. Chen earned a PhD in chemistry from the University of Chicago while Mrs. Chen worked as a journalist with a background in economics. They would meet in New York City with other ethnic Chinese from all over Asia, including Singapore, Hong Kong, and the Philippines, where my own parents are from.

It was the Vietnam era, and Mr. Chen and his friends were young activists who couldn't understand why relations between the United States and mainland China were frozen and trade embargoed. At the time, mistrust and fear between the countries were at an all-time high and the average American had little to no knowledge of what was happening behind Mao Zedong's "Bamboo Curtain." Mr. Chen felt that if his new neighbors in New York City just got to know Chinese

governments couldn't see eye-to-eye, ordinary New Yorkers could at least build trust on a local level with tasty snacks, beautiful crafts, and useful household goods.

But there was one big obstacle: how to bring in embargoed goods when trade with China was forbidden. My father-in-law found a way—several, in fact. One September day—and here he is necessarily vague even after all these years—he drove out to the pier in Red Hook, Brooklyn, to pick up a shipment of what would become Pearl River's first inventory: bottles of soy sauce, copies of Mao's *Little Red Book*, cotton kung fu slippers, and People's Liberation Army caps. There may have been some payments to longshoremen involved. He brought these goods to a tiny Catherine Street storefront they had rented for $600 a month, and boom, Pearl River Mart was born. In the months after, several times a week Mr. Chen would also drive eight hours to Montreal, pick up goods, and then turn right around. He did this with zeal, knowing that those long hours spent in the scorching-hot or freezing-cold truck were serving a larger purpose.

BY THE TIME I ENCOUNTERED PEARL RIVER, IT had already moved to its fourth location, on the second floor of a big brick building on Canal Street and Broadway. As a Chinese American kid growing up in Astoria, Queens, amid mostly Greek and Italian neighbors, I vividly remember the pathologically regular trips to Chinatown with my parents on the weekends. I don't think we ever missed a Sunday.

people and see how beautiful and noble Chinese culture was, that bridges would be built, friendships would form, and discrimination would cease.

Mr. Chen came up with the idea of opening a "friendship store," a place where people of all backgrounds could interact face-to-face and enjoy goods from mainland China. Even if their respective

I would have preferred attending Greek dance classes like all of my friends, but these weekly pilgrimages were nonnegotiable and, unbeknownst to me, forming the foundation for who I am today. My father, who was Chinese but raised in the Philippines, had grown up hearing and reading about wondrous tales of the motherland and imparted a strong sense of Chinese pride to me. Whereas some kids disdained their Chinese heritage, I embraced it, even if only out of loyalty to my dad. Now that he is no longer with us, I feel thankful to have spent so much time both in Chinatown and China with him. I still imagine I see him every so often when I pass certain jaunty older gentlemen on the street.

To get into the city from Astoria, we'd take the N train, which stopped at Canal and Broadway. Since Pearl River was just above the station on the second and third floors, we used Pearl River as a designated spot to meet up before heading home—this was, of course, back before cell phones or even beepers. My sister and I would often luck out and have time to browse around while waiting for other family members.

Pearl River was a wondrous place for a kid. There was candy, toys, stationery, useful household gadgets, clothing and shoes, curiosities, straight-up weird stuff, even weapons! Definitely not your run-of-the-mill, corporate-owned department store. And there were white people there too! Seeing non-Chinese people in Chinatown was not really a common sight at the time. As I grew older and more independent in high school and college, I would still pop in for some of my favorite items, like Bee & Flower soaps, soft cotton Mary Jane slippers, beautiful ceramic bowls, and small furniture items.

While I was an undergrad at Columbia, I met my now husband, Gene. Our friends all thought it was fun that his family owned Pearl River, and over the years most of us had dropped by and gotten to know his parents well. When the store moved from Canal Street to SoHo, I just remember how ENORMOUS it felt. When we would come in to say hello and ask for his parents, it would often take fifteen minutes before one of the staff would be able to locate them in the cavernous space, which felt like three football fields stacked on top of one another. Pearl River was an institution and an indelible part of the experience of living in New York City. Everyone has a story about moving to New York City and discovering Pearl River.

Then 2015 came and the prospect of a New York City without Pearl River felt a little like losing a family member. When the news hit, all the local broadcast and print outlets covered it. The *New York Times* ran not one but two pieces, and even *Vogue* paid tribute. Social media exploded in surprise, sadness, and anger that yet another longtime NYC institution was falling as a result of rising rents and greedy landlords.

It was shocking to us as well. My in-laws never talked much about the inner workings of the store, and if they were going through hard times, they never showed it. We, like most of their customers, took for granted that this quirky, proudly independent icon of a store that so many of us had grown up with—one that had survived 9/11, SARS, Hurricane Sandy, and multiple recessions—might not be around for our own kids.

As an Asian American, the loss was a double whammy. Our community had so few institutions as old and big and established as Pearl River, and almost none that had reached its level of crossover appeal. Over five decades, my in-laws had quietly supported so many in the Chinatown community. Over the years they hired hundreds of new immigrants who were able to springboard into society after gaining their bearings while working with dignity and under equitable conditions. For the homesick who wandered in looking for a small piece of home, they found it, often along with conversation, advice, and a hearty slap on the back in farewell. Even when times were lean, my in-laws gave what they could to support every charity or fundraiser that asked for donations. Five decades of building community and the American dream, but with Chinese characteristics and a New York edge.

My husband and I were just getting our lives back in order after the dizzying one-two punch of having two kids in three years. Work was stable, the kids were both in preschool, and one day soon, we were looking forward to going to the gym more than once a year. After college, I had earned a law degree and a master's in political science, and over the years, I had built a varied career as an attorney, adjunct professor, nonprofit executive, and communications and branding professional. In 2015, I was part of the leadership team at the historic all-women's Barnard College, serving as counsel to the president and vice president for communications. I ran a team of fifteen and was one of half a dozen people in charge of all day-to-day operations.

When I decided to join Pearl River as its president, I had no real idea what I was doing. I had no business or retail experience. I don't even enjoy shopping. What I did have, though, was old-fashioned street smarts, experience running projects and teams, and, like the Chens, a passion for building community. I was also a young parent who recognized that I was in a unique position to save an institution for the next generation of Asian American kids looking for role models and a place to feel proud of their culture.

In November 2016, we reopened the store in a new location at the intersection of Chinatown, Tribeca, and SoHo. A year later, we opened a second store in Chelsea Market, the nation's number one food hall and one of New York's top tourist destinations. A year after that, we partnered with the esteemed Museum of Chinese in America to relaunch their museum store, MOCA Shop by Pearl River. By the time this goes to print, we should have opened our fourth store, the food-focused Pearl River Mart Foods.

So much has happened since we reopened in 2016. We've updated and expanded our inventory. Designed our own original brand of merchandise. Built an art gallery to exhibit Asian American artists, many of whom have continued on to leave day jobs and pursue art full-time. Collaborated with emerging designers, authors, and entrepreneurs to highlight their books, products, and projects. Hosted parties, tastings, and performances that were friendly to multiple generations and made people smile and proclaim their love for New York City. Celebrated Lunar New Year on the local news and smack-dab in the center of iconic Chelsea Market. Rehauled our digital efforts and created content that Asians in Des Moines, Toronto, and Sydney could access and, in so doing, become a part of our community. Supported political candidates to try to vote more Asian Americans and people of color into office.

People ask how I have the energy to do all that we're doing. I tell them I'm running like the devil is chasing me. Owning a small business is maddening, period, and New York City is probably one of the worst places to be a small business owner today. It's frustrating to compete against the likes of Amazon and a rapidly growing sector of venture-capital-backed e-commerce startups. The same people who make most of their purchases on Amazon because of free shipping, convenience, or lower prices will often be the first to respond angrily when their neighborhoods turn into desolate strips filled with empty storefronts and chain pharmacies. Thinking of my in-laws' fifty years of backbreaking work and sacrifices, it makes me want to scream: "Support the small businesses you love! They built our communities, not Jeff Bezos!"

I'm not quite sure what the future holds for us. My short-term goal is to get us to our own fiftieth anniversary in 2021. Whatever happens, though, I know my soul will rest easier than if I'd never tried. As long as Pearl River is around, we're going to lift as many Asian Americans and New Yorkers as we can. We're going to continue standing tall, as a pillar in the community and a place that makes the world a little smaller and a whole lot brighter. Pearl River's mission is not yet complete. And we're not stopping now.

RICE

FROM LEFT TO RIGHT: Sticky Rice with Chinese Sausage (p. 131);
Shrimp and Egg Fried Rice (p. 129)

The funny thing about fried rice—which we do so well at Nom Wah—is that it was traditionally a leftover dish, a way to repurpose extra or day-old rice. Hanging out with its friends in the wok, the cold cooked rice emerges renewed, rich with wok hei, resurrected. But at Nom Wah, plain cooked rice isn't part of the dim sum repertoire—it's not something we serve. So to make our beloved fried rice, we end up buying rice, cooking it, cooling it, and frying it. It's so delicious, all the fuss is worth it. However, if I were you, I would bookmark these recipes next time you order takeout. They always give you way too much rice anyway. Then, the next night, make one of these fried rice dishes, exponentially more delicious than whatever General Tso's you had the first go around.

The following recipes are just suggestions. The beauty of fried rice is that you can toss pretty much whatever you want, whatever you got, in it: rotisserie chicken, broccoli, bacon, carrots, squash! Just make sure that whatever you want to go in there is already prepped by the time the wok gets going. Fried rice is no gentleman: he waits for no one and reaches completion in a few minutes.

EGG FRIED RICE

SERVES 6

Egg fried rice is the OG fried rice. In 600 AD, the culinarian Xie Feng mentions it in his book *Shi Jeng* (*The Book of Food*) as "broken golden rice." The gold likely refers to the eggs that stud the rice.

4 cups cooked white rice
4 tablespoons neutral oil, plus more if needed
5 large eggs, beaten
1 medium Spanish onion, finely chopped
½ cup snow pea shoots
2 teaspoons salt
1 teaspoon sugar
½ teaspoon ground black pepper
2 tablespoons dark soy sauce
2 scallions, finely chopped

LET the cooked rice sit uncovered in the fridge overnight to dry out. When ready to cook, gently toss the rice to loosen it up.

HEAT a wok over medium heat. Add 1 tablespoon of the oil. When oil is shimmering, add the eggs and scramble to whatever consistency you desire. Remove and set aside.

ADD the remaining 3 tablespoons oil to the wok, along with the onion, snow pea shoots, and salt. Cook for a minute or two, until the onions are translucent. Add the rice, tossing constantly, followed immediately by the sugar, black pepper, soy sauce, and scrambled egg. Cook, stirring, for 1 minute, or until the rice starts to get crunchy. Add more oil if needed, if the rice looks dry or to help develop a crust. Top with the scallions and serve immediately.

VARIATION:
SHRIMP AND EGG FRIED RICE

1 pound shrimp, peeled, deveined, and patted dry, roughly chopped

BEFORE you cook the egg, boil 1 cup of water in a wok, add the shrimp and cook for 30 seconds to blanch. Follow the instructions as above, adding the shrimp when you add the onion and snow pea shoots.

STICKY RICE WITH CHINESE SAUSAGE

SERVES 6

Sticky, or glutinous, rice is also called sweet rice. We use it for both savory and sweet dishes. Glutinous rice is a variation of regular white rice (*Oryza sativa*) but with a starch that makes it, you guessed it, sticky. This dish, which translates as no mai fan, began as a leftover rice remediation (just like egg fried rice), and (also just like egg fried rice) is so good that we make sticky rice for the express purpose of using it here.

5 dried shiitake mushrooms

1¼ cups dried shrimp

2 cups uncooked glutinous rice

2 tablespoons neutral oil

3 links Chinese sausage, cut into small pieces

1½ teaspoons salt

1 teaspoon Shaoxing wine

1½ tablespoons light soy sauce

2 teaspoons dark soy sauce

1 tablespoon oyster sauce

1¼ teaspoons toasted sesame oil

2 scallions, finely chopped, to garnish

SUBMERGE mushrooms in hot water for 20 to 30 minutes until tender. Remove, drain, and dice. Meanwhile, submerge shrimp in hot water for 30 minutes until rehydrated. Remove, drain, and pat dry.

PREPARE the rice according to the instructions on the package. Set aside to cool.

HEAT the neutral oil in a wok over medium heat. Add mushrooms to the wok along with the shrimp, sausage, and salt and stir-fry for 3 to 5 minutes, until the mushrooms are browned.

ADD the rice to the wok. Lower the heat and stir-fry for another 15 minutes. Add the Shaoxing wine, soy sauces, oyster sauce, and toasted sesame oil and agitate the wok rapidly to mix.

SERVE immediately, topped with the scallions.

RICE

THE GROCERY STORE GODDESS: SOPHIA NG TSAO OF PO WING HONG

I've been going to Po Wing Hong supermarket ever since I was a kid, but I didn't connect with Sophia until after I took over Nom Wah. She was one of the first second-gen kids around my age I knew to rejoin her family's business in Chinatown. Just like me, she brought the experience she'd gained from business school and in the professional world to bear on a deeply personal and idiosyncratic endeavor. So she knew what it was like to balance filial loyalty with best business practice, to try to forge a path forward while not deviating from what was so successful in the first place. Sophia and I are both very active in the local charity scene, so, one day, after running into each other at some CCBA gala or something, I suggested we go yam cha (grab some tea and talk). We immediately bonded over the challenges faced by next-gen owners, specifically the pressure we feel to always show a happy face. In reality, the business of what we do, the challenges from within and without, can be daunting. But in Chinese culture in particular, to readily admit to struggles publicly is unheard-of. One must maintain mianzi, or face. And as the banner-carriers of two iconic businesses in Chinatown, we often feel the weight of an entire community on us. That connection was made many years ago and she's been my friend and business confidante ever since.

Po Wing Hong supermarket was founded by my parents, Patrick and Nancy Ng, in 1980. At Po Wing, we're known for stocking authentic goods from Asia and from America too. We specialize in delicacies including three of the four treasures of the sea: dried sea cucumbers, which we keep in great glass jars; dried abalone; and fish maw, lily-white bladders that are delicious braised and in soups. (We stopped selling the fourth treasure, shark fin, years ago.) Though much of our product comes from the sea, we also sell rare Chinese products like blood bird's nest, literal strands of nutritionally rich swiftlet saliva harvested in iron-rich caves of China, dried wood ear mushrooms, and cordyceps, or caterpillar fungus. We stock high-quality domestic products like ginseng that is hand-harvested in Wisconsin. We also carry an entire pharmacopeia of traditional Chinese medicine including sek huk (石斛, stone bushel stem), bark of the Eucommia tree; lo hon gwo (羅漢果), the fruit of the monk tree; and much, much more. Other than that, we have everything a normal grocery store has: mops, ketchup, trash bags, and so on. For many of our customers, we are the direct link back to the

kitchens of their childhood, a connection to the herbal remedies of their families.

It has also been my connection to my family. When my parents first opened the grocery, they lived next door from the original location on 148 Hester Street. But Chinatown back in the '80s wasn't anywhere to raise a family, so when I was very young, we moved out to Livingston, New Jersey, a very white suburb where I was one of only two or three Asian kids in the whole community. Like every other Chinese kid, growing up I came to Chinatown every weekend for Chinese school at CCBA, the Chinese Consolidated Benevolent Association, where I learned Cantonese after seemingly endless exercises. After Chinese school, I'd come work here at Po Wing, stocking shelves, practicing my Cantonese with the staff and customers, and feeling generally at home.

In fact, in the aisle and back office of Po Wing is where I saw the most of my mom and dad. Because the retail business is a hard one with long hours, my parents were hardly ever home. Often they left before I woke up and returned after I had fallen asleep. I was mostly raised by my grandmother, Maa Maa (*grandma* in Cantonese). Maa Maa was a small smiling woman, tucked like a stitch in our home in Livingston, New Jersey. It was about as far away as she could be from where she was born in Guangzhou. Maa Maa was my father's mother, who had in the span of her lifetime endured two brutal wars, the deaths of much of her family at the hands of Mao Zedong's Cultural Revolution, including her husband—my grandfather—and uprooting herself from her

homeland. But of this she never spoke, and I didn't learn any of it until she passed away in 2011.

As I was growing up, the last thing I wanted to do was join the business that had kept my parents from me for so long. Like many second-gen immigrants, I was driven to enter the professional class. I went to Boston University, got a degree in international management, and when I graduated got a job with Federated Department Stores. I moved to Portland, Oregon, eager to live by myself for the first time in my life.

But as time went by, I missed the East Coast. I missed my family, especially my grandmother, who wasn't doing well. And at the same time, my

work as a consultant made me realize just how well run Po Wing was as a business. I'm the middle of three siblings, but it had also become clear that if someone from the family was going to run the business, it would be me. This realization coincided with my parents deciding, very gradually, to take a step back from the business they had built.

When I returned, I was one of the few—in fact, the only that I knew of—kids to come back into the family business by choice. It was lonely, to be quite honest. I was greeted with a lot of raised eyebrows. Some people thought I was simply taking advantage of my family's success. Others couldn't understand why I would get *back* into the grocery business, which, after all, is seen as a stepping-stone for so many Chinese families, a stage for a family to move through.

But a few things drew me back to New York and to Po Wing. First, my grandmother, who was nearing the end of her life. Second, I had watched my parents establish themselves in their community for the last twenty years. I had watched them build relationships not only with the suppliers—those cagey ginseng hunters in Wisconsin, the sea cucumber harvesters from South Korea—but with our Chinatown neighbors. To our community the Ng family meant something, and my name meant something to me too. Last, from a professional standpoint, I could see how the changing relationship of the United States and China offered both opportunity and challenges.

When my parents founded Po Wing, they were importing much of their product from small mom-and-pop companies in Hong Kong. By the time I stepped in, we were doing business with large multinational corporations based in mainland China. As we ramped up our wholesale business, exporting Asian products like rice, noodles, and sauces to countries throughout Central and South America including Belize and Costa Rica, these companies wanted to see someone on our side who could speak their language—not Mandarin or Cantonese, but quarterly reports, year-over-year growth, and return on investment. My background in business gave Po Wing Hong a face, a presence, and a spot at the table for the twenty-first century. Putting large corporate structures behind traditional Chinese products is a sign of just how much China and the Chinese economy has changed.

Obviously, stepping back into the business wasn't a one-way street. It's not as if I arrived with all the answers. In fact, if anything, my time in the corporate world gave me more appreciation for how well it was already run. Many of the companies I had seen operated for the short-term gain of their shareholders. It was almost the exact opposite at Po Wing. My parents prided themselves on always being up-front with our clients, clients they'd had for the past thirty years, clients they knew by name and story. Whereas other businesses sometimes passed off lower-quality herbs as higher-quality or (either wittingly or unwittingly) sold counterfeit goods, my parents always took the extra step to ensure that what we sold at Po Wing was the best we could find. They figured that this high level of trust, earned over decades, was the key to long-term success. And it has been.

Like many Chinese families, they were also heavily involved in the community, through donating and volunteering at numerous family associations as well as groups like the Kiwanis Club and Chinese American Planning Council. During the long days I spent on our second-floor office, surrounded by pictures of my father with everyone from Howard Dean and Hillary Clinton to Donald Trump, I saw how hard he worked not only to keep the shelves full but to entwine Po Wing into our community vibrant and healthy.

Over the last ten years, I've come to understand that my role here isn't to revolutionize what we've been doing since we opened, nor is it to embrace what's always been done with no evolution. My job is to build on the core strengths my family has already established while maintaining our DNA. In some cases, that means pushing to have our products online. It can mean insisting that signage is in both Cantonese and English. As always, it means being responsive to what our customer base desires. Lately it's been creating pamphlets on how to use things like bird's nest: how to soak it, what to add to it, how to cook it. Especially for ABCs (American-born Chinese), who are interested in our delicacies but not might have had the knowledge passed down to them, I see my job as an educator even more than a grocer. Now, more than ever, the values my parents built Po Wing on are the same values that I carry on: honesty, transparency, and trust.

TOP: Pan-Fried Noodles in Superior Soy Sauce (p. 143)
BOTTOM: Garlic Eggplant Noodles (p. 144)

NOODLES

Every culture has its way with and claim on noodles. But China is the undisputed birthplace of these long heaven-sent field-born ribbons. Researchers have found leftover noodles in northwestern China dating back four thousand years ago. Suck on that, Pompeii! Over the next four millennia, noodle development in China had been working up to one moment: this nest of crispy tangled noodles being slid over the worn Formica to you at Nom Wah Tea Parlor, studded with Chinese sausage and pepped up with hot sauce or perhaps simply ennobled by superior soy sauce. That's us, standing on the shoulders of giants, slurping their noodles.

But for real, the greatest contribution the Cantonese kitchen has given to noodledom in my mind is stir-frying them. Stir-frying noodles gives them that indescribable crunch so many find alluring. It's ex post facto al dente. There are thousands of types of noodles throughout China, with broad variations between the wheat- and millet-made noodles of the North to the rice noodles of the South. There are pulled noodles, sliced noodles, square noodles, round noodles, thick noodles, and thin noodles. The only commonality is that they are long, because noodles—like everything in the traditional Chinese kitchen—hold a symbolic value too: as a representation of long life. To this day, when I think of noodles, the first thing that comes to mind is longevity. Here we mostly use thin dried egg noodles called lo mein we pick up from Twin Marquis, though, as you'll see, we make use of the broader ho fun noodles as well.

SZECHUAN TOFU NOODLES

SERVES 4

I didn't grow up in the era of Szechuan peppercorn, which, though it has been used for millennia in Szechuan cuisine, only recently became an it-ingredient in the States. But man, am I happy it's trendy. The weirdo tingly tangly feeling in the mouth is thanks to the hydroxy alpha sanshool, which makes your brain feel like your cells have been all shook up (as opposed to capsaicin, which makes them feel like they're burned). It's also responsible for the deliciousness of this dish, which makes use of sambal oelek as well, for some good ol'-fashioned mouth burn plus—and let's be honest, this is the secret—an irresistible mix of fried spices suspended in oil from Guizhou.

2 tablespoons light soy sauce

1¼ teaspoons cornstarch

1 tablespoon neutral oil

¼ cup diced Spanish onion

¼ cup minced garlic

1 cup (½-inch) cubed firm tofu

⅓ cup Lao Gan Ma's Spicy Chili Crisp

1½ teaspoons sambal oelek

2 teaspoons light brown sugar

3 tablespoons white vinegar

¼ cup Edamame Dumpling Broth (page 51)

½ teaspoon mushroom powder

½ teaspoon Szechuan peppercorns

½ teaspoon chili powder

1 pound Chinese lo mein noodles, cooked

2 scallions, finely chopped, for garnish

10 to 15 fresh cilantro leaves for garnish

4 or 5 pickled red chilis, chopped, for garnish

1 teaspoon fried garlic for garnish

IN a small bowl, combine the soy sauce and cornstarch to form a slurry.

HEAT the neutral oil in a large saucepan over medium-low heat. Add the onions and garlic and sweat for 5 minutes without developing any color. Add the tofu to the pot and stir to combine. Cook for 5 minutes.

ADD the chili crisp, sambal oelek, brown sugar, vinegar, broth, mushroom powder, Szechuan peppercorns, and chili powder. Increase the heat to medium-high and bring to a boil, stirring frequently. Add the cornstarch slurry and bring the mixture back to a boil, stirring frequently.

TURN off the heat and pour the sauce over the noodles. Garnish with scallions, cilantro, pickled chilis, and fried garlic.

NOODLES

141

PAN-FRIED NOODLES IN SUPERIOR SOY SAUCE

SERVES 4

Pan-fried noodles go through a two-step tango to reach peak pleasure: first they're quickly boiled and then they're thrown into the wok to get their crispiness. It's in the burning crucible of this wok, endowed with wok hei, that the noodles develop their fragrant satisfying character, commingling under such high temperature with the soy sauce, wine, oil, sugar, and herbs. If anyone asks you which dish embodies Cantonese cooking's high-wire act, it's this one.

4 teaspoons light soy sauce
2 teaspoons dark soy sauce
1 teaspoon toasted sesame oil
½ teaspoon salt
½ teaspoon sugar
1 tablespoon Shaoxing wine
¼ teaspoon ground white pepper
1 lb fresh thin HK-style egg noodles (we use the Twin Marquis brand)
4 scallions, cut in 2-inch long slices
1¼ cup white onion, thinly sliced
3 cups bean sprouts

NOTE: *In our notes on soy sauce (see page 3), we recommended Pearl River Bridge Superior Dark Soy Sauce for dark soy sauce. For an added oomph, we recommend using Pearl River Bridge Superior Light Soy Sauce as your light soy sauce for this recipe.*

MIX the soy sauces, toasted sesame oil, salt, sugar, wine, and white pepper in a small bowl and set aside.

BRING a pot of water to a boil and add the noodles. Cook fresh noodles for about 1 minute (or dried for about 2 minutes). Drain, rinse under cold water, drain again very well, and then pat dry with a paper towel.

HEAT a wok or large pan over high heat and add 1 tablespoon of neutral oil to coat. Add white parts of the scallion and onion to the pan. Stir fry for about 1 to 2 minutes. Add the noodles to the pan. Add the soy sauce mixture and toss continuously for 2 minutes or until the noodles are golden brown. Add the bean sprouts and the rest of the scallions and toss for 1 to 2 minutes, or until the bean sprouts are slightly transparent but still crunchy.

VARIATION:
CHAR SIU NOODLES

FOLLOW the instructions above, adding 6 to 8 ounces chopped char siu (see page 183) along with the scallions.

GARLIC EGGPLANT NOODLES

SERVES 4

Since Chinese eggplant has fewer seeds, it is noticeably less bitter than its fellow nightshades. This makes it the perfect ensemble player in this cast of heat, ginger, and garlic. Though not technically a dim sum preparation, Julie Cole developed the recipe as a mouthwatering and hearty vegetarian option at Nom Wah Nolita, and it's since gone on to be one of the best sellers.

1 to 2 tablespoons neutral oil

1 medium Spanish onion, finely chopped

2 cloves garlic, minced

1 (1-inch) piece fresh ginger, peeled and minced

1 large or 2 medium Chinese eggplants, sliced into ¼-inch rounds

1 tablespoon white miso paste

¼ teaspoon crushed chili flakes

¼ teaspoon ground Szechuan peppercorn

¼ teaspoon ground white pepper

½ teaspoon chili powder

½ cup aji-mirin cooking wine

¼ cup Chinese black vinegar

1 tablespoon sugar

¾ teaspoon kosher salt

1½ tablespoons water

4 tablespoons light soy sauce

1 small handful fresh Thai basil, picked off the stems, thinly sliced

1 pound Chinese lo mein noodles, cooked

2 scallions, chopped, for garnish

10 to 15 fresh cilantro leaves, for garnish

4 or 5 pickled red chilis, chopped, for garnish

1 teaspoon fried garlic for garnish

HEAT the neutral oil in a large pot over medium heat. Add the onion, garlic, and ginger and cook for 1 minute, stirring constantly.

ADD the eggplant, reduce the heat to medium-low, and cook, stirring, for 10 minutes, or until the eggplant is cooked through (look for the eggplant to appear slightly translucent and no longer white). If the mixture appears dry, add 1 tablespoon neutral oil to moisten.

ADD the miso paste, crushed chili flakes, ground Szechuan peppercorn, white pepper, and chili powder. Stir to combine and cook for 1 to 2 minutes.

ADD the aji-mirin, black vinegar, sugar, salt, water, and soy sauce and bring to a boil over high heat. Lower the heat back to medium and simmer for 10 minutes, stirring occasionally.

REMOVE from the heat. Pulse the sauce with an immersion blender 2 or 3 times to combine (there will still be chunks). Alternatively, take 2 cups of the sauce and pulse in a blender 1 or 2 times, return the blended sauce to the pot, and stir to combine.

TOP the noodles with the sauce mixture and garnish with basil, scallions, cilantro, pickled chilis, and fried garlic.

SLOPPY JOE NOODLES
AKA SPICY CHICKEN BOLOGNESE SERVED OVER WHEAT NOODLES
SERVES 4

To get from Italy to China, you have to cross the Ionian Sea, the Black Sea, Greece, Turkey, the entire Middle East, and the Caucuses. To get from Little Italy to Chinatown, you have to cross Delancey Street. No wonder our foods have become as entwined as . . . a bowl of spaghetti or lo mein. Noodles are noodles are noodles, and in this preparation, we were inspired by the pasta alla Bolognese offered at nearly every one of the Italian joints that line Mulberry and Mott Streets. Of course, we've added our own touches, replacing Calabrian chilis with Szechuan peppercorns, beef with chicken, and killing the tomatoes entirely. The spirit's there, though, and it comes through the bowl clearly.

2 tablespoons neutral oil

½ Spanish onion, finely chopped

2 cloves garlic, minced

1 (1-inch) piece fresh ginger, peeled and minced

12 ounces ground chicken thigh

2 tablespoons white miso paste

½ teaspoon crushed chili flakes

¼ teaspoon ground Szechuan peppercorn

¼ teaspoon ground white pepper

½ teaspoon chili powder

3 tablespoons aji-mirin cooking wine

1½ tablespoons Chinese black vinegar

2½ teaspoons sugar

¾ teaspoon kosher salt

¼ cup water

1½ teaspoons light soy sauce

½ teaspoon cornstarch

1 pound Chinese lo mein noodles, cooked

2 scallions, sliced, for garnish

10 to 15 fresh cilantro leaves for garnish

4 teaspoons pickled red chilis for garnish

1 teaspoon fried garlic for garnish

HEAT the neutral oil in a medium pot over medium heat. Add the onion, garlic, and ginger and sweat for 1 minute, stirring constantly. Do not let them develop any color. Add the ground chicken and cook, stirring, for 5 minutes, or until the chicken is cooked through.

ADD the miso paste, crushed chili flakes, ground Szechuan peppercorn, white pepper, and chili powder. Stir to combine and cook for 1 to 2 minutes. Add the aji-mirin, black vinegar, sugar, salt, and water and bring to a boil over medium heat.

MEANWHILE, in a small bowl, whisk the soy sauce into the cornstarch to create a slurry.

ONCE the mixture in the pot is boiling, add the cornstarch slurry and return to a boil, stirring occasionally. Remove from the heat.

USE an immersion blender to pulse the mixture 2 or 3 times to combine. Alternatively, take 1 cup of the mixture

and pulse in a blender 1 or 2 times, making sure to maintain the texture of the chicken (do not blend into a smooth paste). Return the blended mixture to the pot and stir to combine.

TOP the noodles with the sauce mixture and garnish with scallions, cilantro, pickled chilis, and fried garlic.

147

HO FUN NOODLE SOUP WITH CHINESE GREENS

SERVES 4

Of course, not all noodles are lo mein. In this soul-warming noodle soup, we use a freshly made rice noodle from Guangdong called ho fun. They're like a warm, comfy scarf, but for your mouth, and also slippery. You'll also see them listed as *chow fun*, which refers to these noodles after they're cooked in a wok. We used to buy ours from Fong On, that is, before Paul remade the shop focused more on tofu. Now we get them from Kong Kee Food on Grand Street in New York's Chinatown.

1 recipe Edamame Dumpling Broth
(page 51), strained
1 pound yu choy (Chinese greens)
1 pound ho fun noodles, just cooked
2 scallions, sliced, for garnish
10 to 15 fresh cilantro leaves for garnish

HEAT the broth in a pot. Add the yu choy and cook for 2 minutes.

REMOVE the soup and greens to a serving bowl. Add the warm ho fun noodles. Garnish with the scallions and cilantro.

THE MUSEUM MAVEN:
NANCY YAO MAASBACH OF MOCA

The backbone of Chinatown is and will always be working-class immigrants. These immigrants, without control of the English language, with little money, and with few connections outside the Chinese community, are so often overlooked that the fact that they fade away unnamed hardly warrants a mention. But at the Museum of Chinese in America, or MOCA, these are the heroes, the faces on the wall, the subject of study, the objects of veneration. You can see why I'm a huge fan of the place.

MOCA began on the second floor of an old school on Mulberry Street in 1980, the brainchild of two activists, Jack Tchen and Charlie Lai, who believed that without intervention, much of what made Chinatown Chinatown—namely, the memories and traditions of "old-timers"—would be lost. So they began collecting artifacts, oral histories, signs, archives, and family heirlooms, carefully cataloguing and preserving what they collected.

By the time I came into its orbit, in the early aughts, the place had moved to a stunning building on Centre Street designed by the architect Maya Lin. (This was part of a municipal effort to rebuild and restore a Chinatown turned ghostly by September 11.) I was always involved in one way or another, as a caterer, a panel participant, a visitor, a community member. And that participation has increased since 2015, when Nancy Yao Maasbach took over as

president. I've run the New York City marathon for the last two years through the museum, raising over 10 Gs for the organization. We were part of a wonderful exhibition mounted in 2017 called Sour, Sweet, Bitter, Spicy: Stories of Chinese Food and Identity in America.

But I never really got to sit down to talk to her about her life. It was, I found, both different from and very similar to mine. That's one reason, perhaps, that we've both devoted our professional lives to rendering the nameless named, honoring those who came before us, and preserving the history of Chinatown that came before us for future generations.

My father is ninety-one years old. He arrived in the United States from Shanghai in 1953. My mother's family is from Shandong, but my mother was born in Chongqing, Szechuan, because of the civil war. My mother is one of ten children. Her father was a general of the Kuomintang Army and, as the Communist forces advanced, the family was pushed south. After the Kuomintang lost the civil war, the family caught the last boat out of China to Taiwan before the Communist takeover. I was amazed to learn that most of the Kuomintang generals lived along the same row of houses in Taipei on Songjiang Road; not surprisingly, there was limited interaction

陳
Maggie E. Fong
Hong Kong
San Francisco, California
劉
Ying Lau
New York
Chang
宮
Kung Chi-Kuang
Lin Chih-Ching
Shenyang and Hangzhou
Flushing, New York
姚
William Tse
伍
Richard Tak Eng
Guangdong, Taishan

Queens. At the age of seventeen, my father moved to Hong Kong to seek employment; he would then move to Taiwan and then back to New York. In Hong Kong, my father slept on a cot in a residential hallway and worked twelve hours a day. Finally, he scraped up enough savings for airplane fare to New York. He entered as a skilled typesetter working for his Uncle Pan. When he arrived, he shared a one-bedroom apartment with three other Chinese American bachelors on 116th Street in the Upper West Side. With good English skills and bookkeeping knowledge, he secured a position at United Artists, but the glamour of the job was lost on him. I remember he mentioned that the staff received tickets to attend the Oscars the year Elizabeth Taylor won for *Who's Afraid of Virginia Woolf?* but he gave the tickets away. "No interest," he said. He was, however, interested in finding a wife.

My mother's family had limited connections. A family friend who liked to play matchmaker suggested that photos of my mother and her three sisters be sent to an eligible Chinese bachelor living in New York. My mom was clearly the cutest with the warmest eyes. She was twenty-six. He was forty. Seeking less adventure and more the American dream and hoping to help her struggling family in Taiwan, my mother settled into a small co-op apartment in Jackson Heights in 1966. My brother was born there in 1968; I was born four years later, in 1972. Our only family in America was Uncle Pan and his family. Uncle Pan gave me my Chinese name: Yao Nanxun. *Nanxun* means a southern fragrance, but for simplicity, everyone called me Nancy. As a young girl, I always felt that

and the war was rarely discussed. I understand now that they had lost the mainland. I wonder if they waited and waited for an unfulfilled wish to return to the mainland but died waiting.

My father, meanwhile, had come from an academic, more established Shanghai family. My father was raised in large part by his uncle, Pan Gongzhan, given my grandfather's early passing. Uncle Pan was a committee member of the Shanghai Municipal Government and the editor-in-chief of the *Shanghai News*. After the civil war, Uncle Pan and his family immigrated to Fresh Meadows,

I was much more complex a person than a simple name like Nancy could represent. The contradiction reminded me how so many Chinese restaurants have beautiful, evocative names in Chinese like "100 Treasures of Old China" but in English the names reads "Magic Wok." Same thing. I'm just Nancy.

When we were growing up, Flushing was not yet "Flushing." Every Sunday, we traveled the twenty minutes into Chinatown over the Kosciuszko Bridge to buy our weekly groceries and get real Chinese food. In our Dodge Aspen, we would drive over the bumpy gratings of the Williamsburg Bridge until we hit the Lower East Side, which was then rather dangerous. My parents would remind us to roll up the windows until we reached the lighting and chandelier stores on the Bowery. That's when we knew we were close to Chinatown. We'd go south on Bowery until we hit the police parking lot at the Municipal Plaza, where we, like every other Chinese family coming into the city, would park for free.

I loved those visits to Chinatown. Back in Flushing I was one of only four Chinese kids: it was me and my brother, Jimmy, and Wendy and Kevin Lee. The Lee family owned the Chinese restaurant on Main Street. Arnold Chu arrived in sixth grade from Hong Kong; I can still hear the mocking singsong: "Nancy and Arnold sitting in a tree K-I-S-S-I-N-G." We were the only two Chinese kids in the sixth grade. In the eyes of my classmates, we were destined to be together because we were both Chinese. In Chinatown, however, there were grocers with fresh produce, schools with classes full of Chinese kids, and—as I got older—long-haired bad boys who drove around in Camaros and smoked Parliaments.

Like a lot of immigrants, my parents hustled hard, which left me to look out for myself. My dad was an accountant at Pan Am for thirty-seven years. The pay was not great, but the benefits were priceless. We were able to travel to Hong Kong and Taiwan for free every summer to visit family and friends. Professionally, my mother was an entrepreneur. She sold Rubik's Cubes, invested in real estate, taught Chinese, sold medical supplies and key chains, went to flea markets searching for treasures, and played lotto every week. She really wanted to be financially successful but did not have a clear guidebook, so she tried many businesses, even a pizzeria in Corona, Queens. She makes a great pizza. Trying to earn my own money and not be a burden on my parents, I held more than ten part-time jobs by the time I turned eighteen. I did everything from making bagels at David's Bagels in Flushing, laying out ads for the *Queens Tribune*, working the register at the Gap, and waiting tables at Bob's Big Boy.

Throughout my childhood, I felt the pressure of my parents to succeed and, from the outside, I did. My family thought I won the golden ticket when I received admission to Hunter College High School on the Upper East Side. Unfortunately, I had trouble acclimating and fell apart on the inside. Thrust into the world of white privilege by parents who had no idea how that world worked, I struggled to adjust. I did well for the most part, but gaining acceptance took me away from studying,

which I would regret for a number of years. I was active as student body president, cocaptain of the softball team, and in other extracurricular activities that I thought I should pursue rather than areas I wanted to naturally pursue. I managed to graduate high school without admission to Harvard, which, odd as it may sound, probably was the intention of any good Asian American kid at Hunter in the 1980s. I attended Occidental College in Los Angeles on scholarship. For two years, I wore Doc Martens in sunny California. It took me a while to adjust.

I spent many years away from New York and my family. I worked for Goldman Sachs in Hong Kong, living the life of an expatriate. I had received my MBA from Yale School of Management and returned to Yale to work as the executive director at the Yale-China Association, a nonprofit dedicated to grassroots relationship building between the United States and China through programs in education, health, and the arts. I received a call in 2015 to serve as president of the Museum of Chinese in America (MOCA).

Apart from the back-end challenges of running an arts and cultural institution in the global arts center of New York City—consolidating donor databases, fundraising, team management, exhibition planning, and the like—my biggest challenge at MOCA is how to keep the museum part of the community and the community part of the museum. Like Wilson said, it's true that many Chinese Americans, especially the older ones, tend not to want to dwell on the past, especially if there are skeletons in the closet. Yet the knowledge of the past is one of the most precious gifts we can pass on. Much of what we do at the museum is find ways to open our doors, whether it's offering free admission to neighborhood residents or partnering with organizations like the Chinese Consolidated Benevolent Association (CCBA), New York Chinese Cultural Center, and Pearl River Mart to highlight local culture. In many ways, I feel like I am making up for my own lost time and recognition of my ancestry and my stories. For so much of my life, I took for granted the struggles, triumphs, and details of my family's immigrant journey. And yet the fact that I'm here, the fact that I've had the life I've been able to lead, the fact that the museum is here, that Chinatown is as vibrant as it is—all of it relies on our ability to keep these stories alive. And they only live if they are told and only remembered if people listen.

TOP: Shrimp Balls (p. 160)
BOTTOM: Shimp and Bacon Balls (p. 160)

BALLS

The pleasure of balls (yuk) is self-explanatory to anyone who has eaten them. They are pleasant to hold. Easy to eat. A cinch to make. Chinese people being Chinese people, there's also some vague association with them bringing good luck during Chinese New Year. But we make balls year-round.

Balls are essentially Master Fillings that have moved out and are living off in the world alone, without the codependence on a wrapper. Shrimp Master Filling, I'm so proud of you! The secret is a good flour dredge and a well-maintained oil temperature to turn them golden brown. Balls also, by the way, make a cameo later in the book, in the Dessert chapter—but it's important to note those balls and these balls share only shape and name. While those conform to the traditional filling and wrapper duality, these are free from all such notions.

>> **CLOCKWISE FROM TOP-LEFT**: Plain Cheung Fun (p. 87); Steamed Shrimp Bean Curd Skin Rolls (p. 95); Chicken Feet (p. 171); Fried Shrimp Crab Claw Balls (p. 163)

SHRIMP BALLS

MAKES 20

1 recipe Shrimp Master Filling (page 42)
3 cups all-purpose flour
Neutral oil for frying

FORM the filling into twenty 1½-inch balls. Sift the flour into a large bowl and lightly dredge the balls one at a time in the flour. Place the dredged balls on a parchment paper–lined baking sheet as they are ready. It's best to dredge right before frying.

WHILE you're forming the balls, fill a deep pot or wok with enough oil to submerge the shrimp balls. Heat to 375°F over medium-high heat.

WORKING in batches of 3 to 5 and making sure they don't touch, fry the shrimp balls for approximately 10 minutes, until golden brown. Remove from the oil with a spider, drain the shrimp balls on paper towels, and serve immediately.

VARIATION:

SHRIMP AND BACON BALLS

But why, I wonder, would you ever have shrimp balls when you can have shrimp and bacon balls? For this variation, simply wrap each shrimp ball with a half strip of bacon before it goes into the flour dredge. The bacon adheres to itself, like pork Velcro.

» TOP-RIGHT: Shrimp and Bacon Balls;
BOTTOM: Shrimp Balls

FRIED SHRIMP CRAB CLAW BALLS
MAKES 20

The fried crab claw is basically a shrimp ball with a crab claw handle. It's like a seafood lollipop. This preparation most likely trickled down from fancier teahouses and banquet halls where the entire ball was likely made of crab meat. It's kinda like how paper doilies remind you of real lace—it's a gesture toward luxury. Today it's common to simply stick the crab claw—we buy our snow crab cocktail claws from Tanners Seafood, an online shop—into a shrimp ball and fry as per normal. This isn't to say, by the way, that the claw is simply cosmetic. After the coating has been eaten, the already-peeled exposed crab claw is yours for eating. A small but delightful bit of meat will reward you.

> 1 recipe Shrimp Master Filling (page 42)
> 3 cups all-purpose flour
> 6 large frozen snow crab claws, thawed
> Neutral oil for frying

FORM the filling into twenty 2½-inch balls, placing them on a parchment paper–lined baking sheet as you go. Sift the flour into a large bowl and lightly dredge the balls, one at a time, in the flour. Stick a crab claw, base side first, into the center of each ball so the pincers are sticking out. Secure the filling with the opposite hand by pressing it firmly around the base of the claw. Place the dredged balls on a parchment paper–lined baking sheet as they are ready. It's best to dredge right before frying.

WHILE you're forming the balls, fill a deep pot or wok with enough oil to submerge the shrimp balls. Heat to 375°F over medium-high heat

WORKING in batches and making sure they don't touch, fry the balls for 13 to 15 minutes, until golden brown. Remove from the oil using a spider, drain the balls on paper towels, and serve immediately.

EGG FRIED RICE ARANCINI WITH SAMBAL KEWPIE

MAKES 25 ARANCINI

Whether this is a ball or fried rice was the cause of much debate within the Nom Wah family—debate that stretched for hours on end and finished when I said, "Meh, I think ball." For her part, though, Julie Cole, who developed the recipe in collaboration with the schmancy members' club Soho House for a high tea, thinks they're egg fried rice. Well, just like sometimes a very new raisin is a very old grape, sometimes egg fried rice in ball form is both things at once. That's called a dialectic.

FOR THE ARANCINI:
2¼ cups sweet potato starch
¼ cup Chinese pork seasoning, Tomax brand recommended
1 teaspoon kosher salt, plus more for sprinkling
1 teaspoon ground black pepper
1 teaspoon garlic powder
6 large eggs
4 cups panko breadcrumbs
5 cups Egg Fried Rice (page 129), cold
Neutral oil for frying

FOR THE SAMBAL KEWPIE:
2 cups Kewpie mayonnaise
½ cup sambal oelek
1 teaspoon kosher salt

FOR THE GARNISH:
¼ cup loosely packed freshly picked cilantro leaves

TO MAKE THE ARANCINI:

IN a medium bowl, combine the sweet potato starch, Chinese pork seasoning, salt, black pepper, and garlic powder. Stir gently to combine. Beat the eggs in another medium bowl and put the breadcrumbs in a third bowl.

PUT the egg fried rice in a large bowl, along with about ½ cup of the starch mixture, ½ cup of the egg (about 2 beaten eggs), and ½ cup of the breadcrumbs and stir to combine. Add equal amounts of each mixture, as needed, until the rice adheres to itself but is not visibly wet or very dry/crumbly.

FORM balls of the fried rice mixture about 1 inch in diameter (about half the size of a golf ball). As the balls are formed, place on a plate or sheet tray, leaving space between each, cover with plastic wrap, and refrigerate for 2 hours.

IN a tall, heavy-bottomed pot, heat 2 inches of neutral oil over medium heat to 350°F.

ONE at a time, dip the fried rice balls into the potato starch mixture, then the egg mixture, then the panko, draining off the excess of each component before dipping into the

next. Return them to the tray as they are
coated.

ONCE all of the balls are coated, carefully
drop them in the oil, 4 or 5 at a time. Fry for
3 to 4 minutes, until golden brown. Remove
from the oil with a spider and transfer to a
paper towel–lined baking sheet. Immediately
sprinkle with salt. Repeat until all the
arancini are fried.

TO MAKE THE SAMBAL KEWPIE AND SERVE:
WHILE the arancini are frying, in a small
bowl, combine the mayonnaise, sambal
oelek, and salt. Stir to combine.
SERVE the arancini with the sambal Kewpie
alongside, or use a squeeze bottle to dot the
top of the arancini with the sambal Kewpie.
Garnish with fresh picked cilantro leaves.

THE DIM SUM ROCK STAR:
WUN GAW OF NOM WAH TEA PARLOR

I first met Wun Gaw ten years ago, when I took over Nom Wah. He was always hanging out with my Uncle Wally. I suspect Wun Gaw has known Wally for many years, but it's hard to tell for sure, because Wun Gaw keeps to himself. Maybe that's why he and Uncle Wally get along so well. I know he loves playing cards. I know he is a steady, calm presence in the kitchen who manages to do a crazy amount of work without ever looking like he's in the weeds. His recipes and his kitchen are what keep Nom Wah full of customers. But beyond that, I know little. For the last ten years, we have worked together day in and day out and we've never had a serious argument between us, nor have we had a deep conversation. So I was really happy to finally have an excuse to ask Wun Gaw the questions I've always wanted to ask and get to know this man, who is a huge part of my life, a little better.

I came to the United States in 1980 with nothing. When I arrived, my first job was in a dim sum restaurant. Not Nom Wah—another one on Mulberry and Canal. A hundred tables. A thousand people. I started low, steaming. Now it's a bank.

I was thirty-one years old when I arrived. I fled China because my family was desperately poor. Life in China at the time was very difficult. My family

and I had to live off $10 a month. It was Mao's era, and his ideology was "everything is everybody's." I didn't like that. I spent five years in Hong Kong before I came here. I left my siblings and my mother. My father had already come to the United States in 1958. I was only six when he left. He worked in a Cantonese restaurant in Chicago, and although he made it possible for me to immigrate, I rarely saw him even after I moved here.

In Hong Kong, I had already worked for two years doing dim sum at a place in Mong Kok. Fifty tables. Five hundred people. Dim sum there is different. I had to get in at 5 a.m. because the rush began at 6 a.m. I lived in a dormitory paid for by the restaurant. It was just a large room with a bunch of bunk beds in it. I learned a lot in that kitchen. Everything was fresh. Nothing was ever frozen. Make it. Steam it. Sell it. Make it. Steam it. Sell it. Ten hours a day. Six days a week.

By the time I started working in New York I was used to hard work. Though I started on steam, I quickly moved to rice rolls, then to frying, then to the wok. The boss saw that I didn't mind working overtime and that I never complained. Ten hours a day, six days a week—same as in Hong Kong. In two years, I became the head chef.

Then, through a friend, I met Wally. He said he needed a chef. I said okay. I began working at Nom

Wah in 2011. Many of the recipes are base formulas from my time in Hong Kong. Over the years, I've added some things and subtracted others, according to my taste and the feedback from customers. Today I look around at Nom Wah and the word that best describes what I feel is fulfillment. I feel fulfilled that we have twenty people working in the kitchen and that so many people come from all over to eat here, with these recipes.

Sometimes I think about how I grew up, eating radishes from the nearby farms because that was all we could afford. I think about where I am today. I'm a grandfather now. I'm at the age when I could retire, but I don't think I will. I have two sons: one works at Goldman Sachs and the other is a customs official at JFK. Those are difficult jobs to attain. I don't take any credit. I let my sons do what they wanted as long as they could have a good education. When I was young, before I left China, I used to build houses, not big ones, but small simple houses around my village for fun. I did everything by hand. I'd like to return there one day to see if anyone is living in them, though of course I know it isn't possible. Nevertheless, I feel fulfilled about what I built here at Nom Wah, in New York, in this country. I built a life.

CLOCKWISE FROM TOP: Sweet-and-Sour Pork Chops (p. 178);
Salt-and-Pepper Pork Chops (p. 178); Salt-and-Pepper
Shrimp (p. 176); Sticky Rice with Chinese Sausage (p. 131)

CHEF'S SPECIALS

Not all dim sum abides by the bifurcation of wrapping and wrapped, vehicle and passenger. Chef's specials are what we call everything that defies a category. They are special, and they are made by our chef, of course. But beyond that, they are a varied crew. Some, like the chicken feet, are traditional dim sum snacks. Others, like the pork chops and salt-and-pepper shrimp, are larger-format plates that we've added over the years as our hours have extended dinner-wardly.

CHICKEN FEET

MAKES 20

Sometimes you will hear this ingredient referred to as Phoenix Claws, but it is actually chicken feet (鳳爪). And I get that you may be skeptical of their culinary value, but these crispy chicken feet are actually are delicious, covert vehicles for the subtle sauce they come with. Yes, they are gelatinous and full of cartilage and bones. They are, after all, feet. But Chinese chefs do not waste food—and they turn off-cuts into delicacies. The multistep cooking process—boiling, marinating, and frying—renders the meat tender and succulent. They'll, um, knock you off your feet. I apologize. I, Wilson Tang, apologize for that terrible Dad joke. (But they will.)

20 chicken feet
½ teaspoon salt
1 teaspoon sugar
½ teaspoon rice wine vinegar
1 tablespoon light soy sauce
2 teaspoons cornstarch
Neutral oil for frying
2 cloves garlic, finely chopped
2 scallions, finely chopped
1½ teaspoons oyster sauce
2 star anise pods
1 tablespoon diced bell pepper, for garnish
5 fermented black beans (dau si), for garnish

USING either a cleaver or kitchen shears, cut off the claws and any dirty or discolored parts of the chicken feet.

BRING a large pot of water to a boil and add the salt, sugar, and rice vinegar. Add the chicken feet and cook for about 2 minutes just to further clean. Remove from the pot using a spider and drain thoroughly.

PLACE the chicken feet in a large bowl. Add the soy sauce and cornstarch, toss to combine, cover, and marinate in the refrigerator for 30 minutes.

FILL a wok or heavy-bottomed pan one third of the way up with neutral oil and heat over medium heat to 350°F. Fill a large bowl halfway with ice and water. Add the chicken feet to the oil and fry until golden, approximately 8 minutes. Using a spider, transfer the feet to the bowl of ice water and leave for 2 to 3 hours. This will make the skin fluffy.

REMOVE the chicken feet from the water. Prepare a steamer according to the instructions on page 10. Add the chicken feet (they should all fit) and steam for 15 minutes.

IN a small bowl, combine the garlic, scallions, oyster sauce, and star anise and pour over the chicken feet. Continue to steam for another 30 to 40 minutes until skin falls easily from chicken feet.

TRANSFER the chicken feet and sauce to a deep pot. Add 1 cup of water to cover the feet and bring to a simmer. Cover and braise for 15 minutes, then remove the cover, increase the heat, and cook for about 5 minutes to thicken the sauce. Garnish with bell pepper and black beans and serve immediately.

STUFFED EGGPLANT

SERVES 4

This is one of my favorite uses of Shrimp Master Filling because it shows how anything can become a wrapper. Take eggplant, for instance. We usually think of eggplant as the filler. We canny Cantonese have made the eggplant into the bun for a shrimpy payload.

8 fairy tale eggplants
1 recipe Shrimp Master Filling (page 42)
1 cup hot water
½ cup oyster sauce
Neutral oil for frying
1 bunch scallions, diced

PREPARE the eggplant by trimming off the stems and ¼ inch from the bottoms. Split lengthwise, cutting two-thirds of the way through.

STUFF each of the cavities with 2 tablespoons of the filling, patting it down well so it won't fall out.

IN a small bowl, prepare the sauce by mixing the hot water with the oyster sauce.

HEAT 3 inches of oil in a Dutch oven to 375°F over medium-high heat. Add the eggplant two at a time and fry for 5 to 7 minutes, until the filling is golden. Transfer to a paper towel–lined plate.

PLACE on a serving platter, drizzle with the oyster sauce, and scatter with the scallions.

SALT-AND-PEPPER SHRIMP

SERVES 4 TO 5

Salt-and-pepper shrimp is a traditional Cantonese preparation and just as simple as it sounds. This is also classic Wun Gaw: Wun Gaw, a man who cooks using only one cleaver and a plastic teaspoon. But as this dish shows, he doesn't need anything else. The alchemy here is in the succulent shrimp, the crispy crust, and the Chinese five-spice powder (a blend of star anise, cloves, cinnamon, fennel, and Szechuan peppercorn). This recipe will give you plenty of salt and five-spice powder to use later.

Neutral oil for frying
1 pound large unpeeled shrimp
(8 to 12 shrimp)
1 tablespoon potato starch
2 tablespoons water
1 teaspoon Chinese five-spice powder
1½ cups kosher salt
1 cup shredded iceberg or romaine lettuce
1 cup shredded carrots

IN a deep skillet or wok, heat 2 inches of oil over medium-high heat to 350°F.

MEANWHILE, use a pair of kitchen shears to cut the shells in order to devein the shrimp (don't remove the shells completely). Trim off the heads if they have them.

IN a large bowl, mix the potato starch with the water until dissolved. Add the shrimp and coat, inside and out, with the mixture.

IN a small bowl, mix together the five-spice powder and salt.

ADD the shrimp to the hot oil and fry for about 2 minutes or until opaque, agitating them after a minute. Transfer to a paper towel–lined plate and pat dry.

MOVE the shrimp to a clean large bowl and toss with 2 tablespoons of the salt and five-spice mixture.

PLACE the shrimp on a bed of lettuce and carrots and serve immediately, along with the extra salt and five-spice mixture for sprinkling.

TOP TO BOTTOM: Salt-and-Pepper Pork Chops (p. 178);
Salt-and-Pepper Shrimp (p. 176)

SALT-AND-PEPPER PORK CHOPS
(AND ITS FRIEND SWEET-AND-SOUR PORK CHOPS)

SERVES 4 TO 6

Wun Gaw once explained to me that he didn't come to the kitchen to fulfill some sort of life passion or to express himself artistically. "That's an American fairy tale," he scoffed. He started working in kitchens because there was nothing else he could do. He used the recipes he knew from back home with the products and proteins available in America. Sweet-and-sour pork chops are a great example, and this recipe proves that delicious doesn't care about the backstory. Even though, admittedly, it can be interesting.

This dish is part of the long lineage of Chinese cooks coming to America and making shit up with what they had. Salt-and-pepper squid is a common preparation throughout China. The salt-and-pepper technique is applied here to pork chops, which are far too extravagant a cut for many cooks in China. After the meat is crispy and crunchy, popping with the flavor from the ample salt and pepper, we run it through a wok with a sweet-and-sour sauce. My favorite thing about it is that it contains A.1. Sauce, the most American of all sauces. I guess that's why sweet-and-sour chops are the most Chinese American of all dishes. They are an addictive main course, with flavors six ways to Sunday.

FOR THE SWEET-AND-SOUR SAUCE
(OPTIONAL):
⅓ cup Koon Chun red vinegar
⅓ cup A.1. Sauce
½ cup honey
1 tablespoon Worcestershire sauce
1½ cups water
Dark soy sauce (optional; only to adjust color if it's too red for your liking)

FOR THE PORK:
1 pound medium boneless pork chops
1½ tablespoons Shaoxing wine
1 teaspoon toasted sesame oil
1 large egg, beaten
½ teaspoon salt
3 tablespoons water

FOR THE COATING:
¼ cup all-purpose flour
2 tablespoons cornstarch
⅛ teaspoon ground white pepper
1½ tablespoons neutral oil
3 tablespoons water

FOR FRYING AND SERVING:
3 cups peanut oil for frying
3 cloves garlic, thinly sliced
3 long hot green peppers, sliced crosswise into thin rounds
1 long hot red pepper, sliced crosswise into thin rounds
½ teaspoon coarse sea salt
⅛ teaspoon coarsely ground white pepper

IF YOU'RE MAKING THE SWEET-AND-SOUR SAUCE:

COMBINE the red vinegar, A.1. Sauce, honey, Worcestershire sauce, and water in a small saucepan. Place over medium heat and bring to a boil, stirring constantly. Adjust the color of the sauce with dark soy sauce, if desired. Turn off the heat and let sit for 10 minutes, or cool completely and store in the refrigerator for up to 2 weeks.

TO MAKE THE PORK AND COATING:

COMBINE the pork, Shaoxing wine, toasted sesame oil, egg, salt, and water in a large bowl, and use your hands to mix and coat the pork evenly. Let sit for at least 15 minutes and up to 2 hours.

MOVE the pork to one side of the bowl, add the ingredients for the coating, and mix until you get a loose batter. Combine the pork with the batter until the pork is well coated and set aside.

TO FRY THE PORK AND SERVE:

HEAT 2 inches of neutral oil in a large cast-iron skillet or Dutch oven to about 250°F, or until a piece of garlic tossed in bubbles a little. Add the garlic and cook until it just starts to turn color, about 30 seconds. Using a spoon, scoop it out onto a paper towel–lined plate to drain. Be careful not to brown the garlic or it will be bitter.

HEAT the same oil to 380°F. Working in batches, add the pork and fry until golden brown, approximately 7 to 10 minutes. Using tongs to remove pork, place on a paper towel–lined sheet to drain.

HEAT a wok over very high heat until smoking. Add the green and red peppers, salt, and white pepper and toss for 15 to 30 seconds, until fragrant.

IF you're going for a sweet-and-sour pork chop, add ½ cup of the sweet-and-sour sauce. If not, just keep on going.

TURN off the heat and add the pork chops and fried garlic to the wok. You can now practice your wok skills to toss everything together. Serve immediately with white rice.

STEAMED SPARERIBS

SERVES 4 TO 5

Gweilo—ahem, white people—never talk about gnawing in a good way. It's always like, "Something is gnawing at me": pains of growing old, the thought of dying alone, maybe I left the stove on? But we Cantonese, we love a good gnaw. There's something so satisfying about working a piece of meat or bone over, extracting from it every morsel of flavor. That's gross, you say, as you twirl your bite-marked pencil between your fingers with your tooth-torn cuticles, and then it dawns on you, maybe you too love the gnaw. Save your fingers and go order the steamed spareribs, in which bone and cartilage and meat are the perfect 1:1:1 ratio. These chewy cubes can be eaten as a snack or within cheung fun or even tossed, if you'd like, with fried rice.

½ teaspoon salt

1 teaspoon MSG

1½ teaspoons sugar

½ teaspoon chicken powder

½ teaspoon ground white pepper

1 tablespoon Shaoxing wine

1 tablespoon toasted sesame oil

2 pounds spareribs, cut into 1-inch by 1-inch segments

2 tablespoons potato starch

1 tablespoon neutral oil

1 teaspoon fermented black beans

¼ large green bell pepper, seeded and roughly chopped

¼ large red bell pepper, seeded and roughly chopped

IN a large bowl, combine salt, MSG, sugar, chicken powder, white pepper, wine, and toasted sesame oil. Mix until uniform.

ADD the spareribs and toss until well coated. Add the potato starch and toss again until coated and, finally, add the neutral oil and toss until coated. Sprinkle with the fermented black beans.

SET up a steamer according to the instructions on page 10. Steam the spareribs on a plate for 18 minutes, or until cooked through.

MEANWHILE, bring a pot of water to boil. Add the bell peppers and blanch for 30 seconds. Remove from the water with a spider and set aside on a paper towel–lined plate to dry.

REMOVE the spareribs from the steamer, drain any excess water, and top with the bell peppers. Serve immediately.

CHAR SIU FAMILY MEAL
SERVES THE KITCHEN STAFF OF NOM WAH (20 PEOPLE)

Family meal at Nom Wah usually consists of cigarettes smoked on the corner of Doyers Street. Most times, the staff will bring their own food from home plus a bit more to share and there's a very informal potluck. But sometimes, when he's in a good mood, Wun Gaw will cook for everyone. The unanimous favorite is char siu, or Chinese BBQ pork. There are plenty of places in Chinatown that specialize in char siu who have rows of the scarlet red–glazed tenderloins hanging in their windows. But it's actually quite easy to make, and—what with the overnight marinade—it's the perfect weekend project. Make your char siu Sunday night and stretch it out over the week with noodles, bao, and char siu fried rice.

1 (6-pound) pork tenderloin
2 teaspoons toasted sesame oil
2 teaspoons Shaoxing wine
1½ teaspoons salt
1 tablespoon MSG
2 tablespoons plus 1 teaspoon sugar
½ teaspoon chicken powder
¼ teaspoon ground white pepper
3 tablespoons light soy sauce
1½ tablespoons oyster sauce
½ cup ketchup
½ cup hoisin sauce
1 teaspoon Chinese five-spice powder
¼ cup yellow food coloring
¼ cup red food coloring

CUT the pork tenderloin into 3 equal-sized pieces and score ¼-inch-deep incisions across the tops.

COMBINE the rest of the ingredients in a large bowl and mix well. Place the pork in the marinade, tossing to coat. Cover and refrigerate for at least 3 hours or overnight.

WHEN ready to cook, preheat the oven to 350°F.

PLACE the pork in a roasting pan and cook for 45 minutes to 1 hour, flipping after the first 20 minutes, until the internal temperature of the pork reaches 145°F.

REMOVE the pork from the oven and let rest for 10 minutes. Slice into ¼-inch strips and serve. (Or use for bao filling; see page 20.)

THE TOFU KID: PAUL ENG OF FONG ON

The original Fong On on 46 Mott Street was part of my weekly Chinatown circuit as a kid. After Chinese school at 62 Mott—where my kids go now—I'd head over there with my mom to pick up soy milk, turnip cakes, sticky rice cakes, and freshly made hot tofu, still glistening and wobbly. It was a cheap place; I remember it being a little bit grimy, but I loved it. Especially during the summer, nothing beat their herbal glass jelly, which is basically Chinese Jell-O made with boiled mint and starch, topped with loads of brown sugar. When I was a kid, their father was behind the counter. When I was a little older, still a teenager, it was David Eng who took over. David was a quiet guy but hardworking. He took up the family mantle. And it was David to whom I turned when I took over Nom Wah. What started as a business relationship primarily—they supplied the rice milk we made our rice rolls with—turned into a mentorship and later friendship. He thought I was crazy but fully supported my jumping back into an old Chinatown business. He knew firsthand all the challenges it held.

I had always taken Fong On for granted, so it came as a shock when the place closed. I should have known. David was getting older. None of his kids wanted to run an eighty-year-old tofu business. Monty, his older brother, had retired as a cop back in 1993 and was tired of rising every morning at 5 a.m. to make tofu. Their father had passed away and their mother was—and is—old. Nevertheless, when the doors closed permanently, I was in shock.

And then I met Paul Eng, the youngest of the Eng brothers. I never knew Paul growing up. He had lived a life well apart from the family business, but I think he, like me, like so many ABCs, saw that his family's legacy was in danger of being snuffed out forever. So he stepped in.

During the year or so before Fong On reopened in 2019, Paul and I would get together occasionally to both commiserate and offer support for carrying on a family business. Like David once thought about me, I thought about him. He was crazy for doing it, but I was very supportive. When the doors finally reopened in July 2019, I was one of the first in line, eager to taste again the glass jelly, the fresh tofu, a taste of my past and of the future too.

Tofu has been made for the last two thousand years. At Fong On, our tofu store on Mott Street, my family has been making it over three generations for the last eighty years. Though I grew up in the business, spending my weekends among vats of silken bean curd and the hum of compressors, I never thought I'd become a tofu maker like my grandfather, Bing-sun Eng, who started the business, or my father, Wun-Hong Eng, who continued, or my elder brothers, Monty, Kivin, and David Eng, who ran it. On the other hand, I never thought I'd need to. I thought Fong On would always be there.

Fong On first opened in 1933. My grandfather wasn't some tofu-obsessed aesthete. He was just a new arrival in a foreign country with no safety net and a family back in China to provide for. Once he got to America, an old sailor named Mr. Law, a friend from Toishan, took him under his wing and taught him the art of making tofu, telling him the market was there. Bing-sun thought why not? Chinatown was full of homesick men just like him. They wanted tofu, a fundamental part of Chinese cooking. They needed tofu. He needed work. So, with two of his friends, he started the business in a tenement building on Mott Street.

Walk into our store today and you'll see a small-scale industrial wonderland. We have stainless steel grinders that turn the soybeans into paste, which is separated into pulp and soy milk. But back then, tofu making was backbreaking labor, made in the same way it had been for millennia. My grandfather ground the soybeans by hand with a stone grinder until they formed a runny paste, which soy milk was extracted from by hand-pressing and straining. Then he added calcium sulfate, which serves to coagulate the liquid. Then he pressed each block into its form by heaving heavy rocks atop a mold until the weight squeezed out the whey. It was a demanding manual process, but by then my grandfather had gotten used to hard work.

By the time he opened Fong On, my grandfather had already lived multiple lives. He was born Fong-On Yee on December 9, 1890, in Toishan. His family was desperately poor and, when he was four years old, his father sold him to a neighboring childless family, the Eng family, for forty ounces of silver. He became Bing-sun Eng. With few opportunities beyond farming, in the spring of 1920, he sought passage on a freighter to Cuba. For two years, he lived in Havana working as a farmer, until sometime in the early 1920s, when he won the lottery. Literally, he won the lottery. Though I don't know how big the jackpot was, he stashed half in Cuba and used the other half to travel back to China with a heavy haul for his family. He cut quite an attractive figure, and my father was born a year later.

In 1933, however, needing work and having run through the money, my grandfather—and two friends—smuggled themselves back into the United States by hiding on a ladder inside a water tanker. It cost him $200 to get here. The rest of his fortune somehow was lost in Cuba. Once in the States, he met Mr. Law, and shortly after, he founded Fong On. A year later, my grandfather happened to meet a guy in the neighborhood, something Chan. Mr. Chan had a son who was supposed to join him in America, but something went sideways and he couldn't come. So Chan sold my grandfather his son's immigration papers and my grandfather swapped out my dad, who was nine years old at the time. My father made the journey on a boat to Ellis Island in 1935 as Gwing Chee Chan on false papers, with Mr. Chan pretending to be his father.

There was no question as to what my father would do for a living. He didn't want to join the business at first. At age nineteen, my father joined the US Army and served in World War II. Though he wasn't deployed abroad, he was assigned to

a tool and die shop and learned a trade. I think he would have loved to become a manufacturer, but when he got back to Chinatown, there was Fong On awaiting. With a family to support and a father to please, my father soon joined the Fong On workforce, which at that time numbered five people and produced over twenty thousand pounds of tofu a year.

That was the world into which I was born in 1966. By that time, Fong On had changed its name to Fong Inn Too. My father had put his manufacturing background to good use and vastly increased our output. He installed a winch and crane and devised a sort of Freddy Krueger set of blades to cut large blocks of tofu into smaller ones. As is the case with so many American-born Chinese children of entrepreneurs, my life had relatively little to do with the business. Now, that's not the same for my four older brothers, the oldest of whom is nineteen years older than me (a full generation) and the closest is eleven years older. By the time I was born, Fong On was fully occupied by Eng children. So my interest turned elsewhere.

I grew up playing computer games and guitar. I studied architecture, went on to design office spaces—not fun—switched to graphic design, played in bands, most notably Piss Factory, moved to Moscow, married and had a kid in Moscow, and only came back in 2014, after Putin snatched power back from Medvedev. It became clear we were living under a new authoritarian regime and that the ruble would crash. I arrived in New York with my wife, Marina, and a kid in tow. I would later add another kid, Ruby, in New York.

What I found at Fong On was alarming. Since my father retired in the early '70s, my older brothers Kivin and David were running the business. But the two didn't see eye-to-eye. David wanted to expand into large-scale wholesale, while Kivin wanted to keep the operation retail. (That's not entirely accurate. My father retired physically from the store but was still active in development. My mother was also a strong force in the store. Both Kivin and David wanted to do larger wholesale business. We were doing wholesale already but wanted to go big. But because of the micromanaging and grip, my parents had quashed any idea of going big.) What that meant is that we had gotten too big for our own good but not big enough because we were unable to make the step toward large-scale wholesale. Meanwhile, our local customer base, really our lifeblood, was growing older and/or leaving the neighborhood. Like so many legacy brands in Chinatown, we were slowly grinding ourselves down, keeping the doors open more to provide safe haven for our employees than to make money.

Then, three years ago, a few weeks before the Chinese New Year, the store on 46 Mott Street closed its doors for good. Business had slowed to a crawl. My mother kept the business going from behind the scenes but was too frail to work. Kivin passed away in 2009 and David himself was getting older. I think everyone in the family was heartbroken—relieved but heartbroken. For my brothers, who had been getting up at 4 a.m. for the last three decades, it was a welcome change. But it felt like we were relinquishing the foothold that brought my family up from poverty to the solid middle class.

I had been watching the fortunes of Fong On from afar, which felt like watching the overarching story of my family slip away. Initially I was too young to fully partake in the business, and by the time I could I was too far away. And now that I was back stateside, the business was gone. I cast about for ways to keep Fong On—our recipes, our traditions—alive. There was still space in the world for Fong On, I thought, though I knew I'd have to act quickly. Despite the closure, the embers of our business were still glowing, but they wouldn't glow forever.

I'm the first Eng in the history of Fong On to walk back into the business in a very long time.

Unlike my grandfather, driven by necessity, and my father and brothers, driven by familial obligation, I chose the business as opposed to the other way around. The only problem was there was no business to choose, at least not yet.

After exploring grant opportunities, I realized that if Fong On were to live, it would be up to me. We still owned the space on 46 Mott Street, though the equipment had been sold off. And we still owned the recipes, technically, but the knowledge was stored in the bodies of our employees, many of whom moved away after we closed the business. Those I found often were vague about quantities.

"How much water should I use?" I asked my cousin. "A cup full" was the answer. "Like 8 ounces?" "No, the one that hung on a nail on the wall." It goes without saying that that cup had been long gone.

So very unexpectedly but quite rapidly, my life was taken over by tofu. I needed not only to teach myself how to make bean curd, but I had to purchase the right machines and find new employees. Since my Chinese isn't very good, I ended up traveling to Taiwan, to the only tofu machine making company I could find with a website in English. I came back with an order of grinders, presses, and extractors.

Just as important, I discovered grass jelly, a delicious Taiwanese snack made by boiling the stalks and leaves of Chinese mint (*Mesona chinensis*) and thickening the result with starch. This is oven served atop bowls of silky, liquidy tofu pudding. Taiwanese eat the snack with toppings like azuki beans, taro balls, tapioca, and brown sugar. I knew that if Fong On was going to be successful, we'd need to expand. And though perhaps my grandfather and father would frown upon including a Taiwanese street food in our repertoire, I'm also certain they'd applaud the innovation. I also made cosmetic upgrades—a counter looking out onto the street and white subway tiles we'd write the various grass jelly toppings on. Tofu, our bread and butter, is available by the cube from a cooled grab-and-go.

When we opened in 2019, the space was full of light and people. I was deeply happy to be able to fulfill my destiny as an Eng to make tofu again. I was happy to be surrounded by the rattle and hum of the machines. I noticed that the customers weren't the old-timers who used to frequent the shop but young, both Chinese and not, often with their phones out, ready to capture whatever we served. This wasn't the Fong On of the past. It is the Fong On of the present, and I'll be holding space for it to be the Fong On of the future, however that looks.

FEASTS

Peking Duck (p. 202)

A couple times a year, Wally has people over to his social club, the Tong On Association. I love it. I'm the youngest guy in the room, and, being forty-one, that's no longer something I get to say very often. The dinner takes place on the third floor in a sort of rec room with eight or nine circular tables. All the old-timers are there, guys Wally has grown old with since he came to New York. Wun Gaw comes over from Nom Wah to hang out too. He's in charge of the kitchen. He plays cards. He smokes. He drinks. It's great to see him let loose a little, and it's fun to see him not making dumplings.

Before he arrived at Nom Wah, Wally worked at a few Cantonese banquet-style restaurants, and here he draws from that repertoire. Some Chinese banquets are formal affairs, proceeding with an elaborate order and full of auspicious symbols. Most, for instance, have eight courses, since eight is considered the luckiest number in China. There's this whole thing about how you as a guest have to compliment the host in a certain way and they have to apologize and yadda yadda yadda. But at Uncle Wally's, everything is pretty freeform. Especially when the Costco-sized bottles of Johnnie Walker Red appear and the hardcore games of Chinese poker start. By then, don't look for Wun Gaw in the kitchen. But before all that, he cooks like a madman. The following recipes come from this off-hours Wun Gaw, Wun Gaw with his boys and among friends.

Banquets like these, by the way, are happening in Chinatown in social clubs and civic associations and at charity events all the time. And it warms my heart. One of the hidden blessings of the Chinese community's longtime battle with discrimination and exclusion from mainstream society is that we've come to rely on one another. Pretty much everything you see in Chinatown, when you scratch the surface, isn't the result of any particular Great Man. Instead, it relies on an interconnected web of alliance and affiliation and interdependence. And these bonds are resilient and still much-needed. In some cases, our ancestors were incredibly successful at integrating into their communities, and the mission of these gatherings is now simply to preserve our culture and traditions. But in many others, these benevolent societies and village-based social clubs still provide lifelines to thousands of immigrants who would otherwise lack a social net. It makes me kinda weepy. Let's talk about walnut shrimp.

WALNUT SHRIMP

SERVES 4 TO 5

This walnut shrimp recipe, which is seriously addictive, will strike a chord in the hearts of any Chinese kid who went with their parents to banquets such as these—banquets that lasted late into the night, way past bedtime. And you still had to go to Chinese school in the morning! Thankfully, walnut shrimp is the kind of recipe that kids go nuts for, so it wasn't all bad. And if you want to know the secret to this dish: it's not exactly "authentic." But in my mind, Wun Gaw is as authentic as it gets, so whatever Wun Gaw makes is authentic. Ergo, this walnut shrimp is worth your time.

¼ teaspoon salt, plus more for boiling the shrimp
Neutral oil for frying
¼ teaspoon MSG
1 pound large shrimp (8 to 12), shelled and deveined
1 large egg white, beaten
1½ teaspoons potato starch
1 tablespoon vegetable oil
1 cup all-purpose flour
1¾ cups water
6 tablespoons sugar
1 cup walnut halves or whole pecans
Florets from 1 head broccoli (approximately 1½ pounds)
1 cup mayonnaise
Juice of ½ lemon

BRING a large pot of salted water to a boil.

MEANWHILE, in a large skillet over medium-high heat, heat enough neutral oil to submerge the shrimp to 350°F.

AS the oil heats, combine the salt and MSG in a large bowl and mix well. Add the shrimp and toss until well coated, then add the egg white and toss again to coat. Add the potato starch to the shrimp and toss to coat once more, and then the vegetable oil and toss to coat a final time.

IN a separate large bowl, mix together the flour and 1½ cups of the water to form a liquidy paste and set aside.

COMBINE the remaining ¼ cup water and the sugar in a small saucepan and bring to boil over medium heat. Reduce the heat and simmer for 3 to 4 minutes to make a simple syrup.

ADD the walnuts (or pecans) to the hot oil and fry for 3 to 5 minutes or until dark brown. Drain on paper towels, then add to the pot of simple syrup. Toss to coat and stir over low heat until there is no loose syrup left in the pan and the walnuts are crunchy. Transfer the walnuts to a plate and set aside.

ADD the coated shrimp to the boiling water until halfway cooked, about 1 minute. Remove from the water with a spider and drain onto a paper towel–lined plate. Quickly blanch the broccoli in the same boiling water, approximately 1 minute. Remove, drain, and set aside.

MAKE sure your frying oil is at 350°F. Toss the shrimp in the flour mixture, then add to the oil and fry for approximately 1½ minutes, until lightly golden. Remove the shrimp from the fryer using a spider and drain onto a paper towel–lined plate.

IN a large bowl, combine the mayonnaise and lemon juice. Add the shrimp and toss until well coated. To serve, place the broccoli florets into a ring on the plate. Spoon the shrimp at the center and scatter with the walnuts.

CANTONESE-STYLE BEEF FILET

SERVES 4 TO 5

What we call Cantonese-style beef filet holds in it an entire story of immigration and colonialization. The dish itself comes from Hong Kong, where largely Cantonese chefs were inspired by the dining habits and ingredients of the West. These included two of the most Western-y things: steak and ketchup. As many of those chefs immigrated to the United States—including Wally and Wun Gaw—they brought this recipe with them.

2 pounds flank steak
¼ teaspoon baking soda
2 tablespoons plus 1½ teaspoons water
1 (2-inch) piece fresh ginger
1½ tablespoons light soy sauce
2 heaping tablespoons potato starch
4 tablespoons neutral oil
½ medium white onion, roughly chopped
1 cup sweet-and-sour sauce (page 178)

CUT the steak in half lengthwise, and then into ½-inch slices on a bias. Using a meat tenderizer, pound each slice of meat to ⅛ inch thick. Pat dry with paper towels.

IN a small bowl, combine the baking soda with 1½ teaspoons of the water and stir to dissolve.

SMASH the ginger with the tenderizer or the flat side of a knife and, using your hand (or a citrus press), squeeze the juice into the baking soda mixture. Add the soy sauce and mix well.

IN a large bowl, toss the meat with 1 heaping tablespoon of the potato starch until evenly coated. Add 3 tablespoons of the neutral oil and toss again to coat. Add the ginger and soy marinade, toss once more, then cover the meat in plastic wrap and let sit, refrigerated, for at least 30 minutes or overnight.

WHEN ready to cook, let the meat come to room temperature, about 30 minutes. Heat a large skillet until very hot. Add the remaining 1 tablespoon neutral oil over high and heat until shimmering. Add the meat and stir-fry for 5 minutes until browned. Remove to a plate and set aside.

ADD the onion to the skillet and cook over high heat for approximately 1 minute, until translucent. Add the sweet-and-sour sauce and toss to coat.

IN a small bowl, combine the remaining 1 heaping tablespoon of potato starch with the remaining 2 tablespoons water. Mix well, then add to the skillet with the onions and sauce. Return the meat to the skillet and mix everything together to combine. Transfer to a platter and serve immediately.

CANTONESE-STYLE TARO AND PORK BELLY CASSEROLE

SERVES 10

Another mid banquet home run, this casserole relies on the complementary flavors and textures of taro and pork belly: one meaty, the other earthy; one chewy, the other tender; one Lilo, the other Stitch. The key is to allow the taro to soften to the cusp of dissolution and make the pork belly crisp on the skin side and melt-in-your-mouth soft on the fat side.

5 pounds pork belly, skin on
1 tablespoon dark soy sauce
1 tablespoon neutral oil
6 pounds fresh taro, peeled and cut into ¼ by 3 by 1-inch slices
1 teaspoon salt
2 teaspoons MSG
4 teaspoons sugar
1 tablespoon Shaoxing wine
1¼ tablespoons toasted sesame oil
¾ teaspoon chicken powder
½ teaspoon ground white pepper
½ teaspoon Chinese five-spice powder
2 cups fermented bean curd

BRING a large pot of water to a boil. Submerge the pork belly in the boiling water for 2 minutes to clean it. Remove from the pot and place in a colander. Rinse under cold water.

USING a siu yuk poker (a needle or skewer works just as well), poke holes in the skin of the pork belly. (This will make the skin crispy after cooking.)

IN a large bowl, toss the pork belly with the soy sauce to coat.

MEANWHILE, heat the neutral oil in a large skillet to 350°F over medium-high heat. Add the pork belly and fry for 2 minutes on each side. Remove from the oil and set aside on a paper towel–lined plate.

MAKING sure your oil is still at 350°F, add the taro (working in batches, if needed) and fry for about 2 minutes, until lightly browned. Remove and drain on a paper towel–lined tray.

ONCE the pork belly is cool enough to handle, cut it into 3-inch strips. Place in a large bowl and mix with the taro.

IN a small bowl, combine the salt, MSG, sugar, wine, toasted sesame oil, chicken powder, white pepper, five-spice powder, and fermented bean curd. Stir until the bean curd is broken up. Pour over the pork belly and taro mixture and toss until coated.

ON a heat-safe tray, alternate tiles of pork belly and taro root, tightly packed. You can use multiple trays. Using the steaming method on page 10, steam the trays in batches for 30 minutes, or until tender.

USING a spatula or your hands, transfer the pork belly to the platter, maintaining the alternating pattern. Pour the remaining sauce on top and serve.

SHIITAKE MUSHROOMS AND LETTUCE

SERVES 6 TO 8

It's rather unusual to find veggie-forward dishes at Chinese banquets since these dishes are associated with austerity. However, this classic Cantonese combination gets the nod because shiitake mushrooms—and mushrooms in general—are associated with good health and longevity. In this astonishingly easy entrée, rehydrated mushrooms are complemented by boiled lettuce and glazed to a high sheen.

2 ounces dried shiitake mushrooms
¼ cup neutral oil
2 cloves garlic, peeled and lightly crushed
4 thin slices fresh ginger, ⅛ inch thick
2 cups chicken broth
1 tablespoon oyster sauce
1 teaspoon sugar
1 teaspoon freshly ground black pepper
1 teaspoon Shaoxing wine
1 teaspoon salt
1 head iceberg lettuce, quartered
1 teaspoon toasted sesame oil
3 scallions, thinly sliced (optional)

SUBMERGE mushrooms in hot water for 20–25 minutes until tender. Reserve soaking water.

MEANWHILE, in a large pot, heat 2 tablespoons of the neutral oil over medium heat. Add the garlic and ginger and cook for 2 minutes, or until fragrant.

ADD the rehydrated mushrooms and cook for an additional minute. Add the chicken broth, oyster sauce, sugar, black pepper, and Shaoxing wine. Bring to a boil and boil for 2 minutes, then lower the heat to a simmer and cook uncovered for 1 hour, stirring occasionally and adding some of the reserved soaking water as needed to maintain a thick sauce.

WHEN the mushrooms are almost done, the flesh will look slightly translucent. Turn off the heat. Fill a pot with enough water to submerge the lettuce and bring to a boil. Add the salt and remaining 2 tablespoons neutral oil. Add the lettuce, cover, and cook for 2 to 3 minutes, until the lettuce is tender. Drain excess water, pat dry with paper towels, and arrange the lettuce leaves on a serving platter.

TURN the heat under the mushrooms back up to medium-high. Add the toasted sesame oil and scallions. Stir for 1 minute, then pour the braised mushrooms onto the bed of cooked lettuce.

PEKING DUCK

SERVES 4

Walk through Chinatown and the eyes of a thousand Peking ducks follow you from their resting place in storefront windows. Making Peking duck isn't easy and it's not part of the dim sum canon—and yet, Julie, our chef at Nom Wah Nolita, had an indomitable curiosity and several strokes of brilliance. She came up with this at-home recipe that avoids the traditional wood-fired oven because, well, who has a wood-fired oven? Miraculously, the conventional oven still achieves the perfect crispiness for the duck. They are traditionally served with mandarin pancakes, but we like to serve them in mantao with hoisin sauce, cucumbers, and scallions.

1 duck (5 to 6 pounds)
1 tablespoon distilled white vinegar
1 gallon hot water
2 tablespoons honey
3 tablespoons oyster sauce
2 tablespoons Chinese five-spice powder
3 tablespoons light soy sauce
2 tablespoons brown sugar
½ cup seeded julienned cucumber, for garnish
½ cup julienned scallions, for garnish
½ cup hoisin sauce for serving
Mantao (page 19) for serving

PRICK the duck all over the whole surface with a fork, piercing the skin but not the flesh. This yields a crispy skin.

IN a bowl large enough to fit the duck, mix the vinegar with the hot water. Place the duck in the bowl and soak for 5 minutes.

TRANSFER the duck to a wire rack to drain and pat with paper towels until extremely dry.

IN a small bowl, mix together the honey, oyster sauce, five-spice powder, soy sauce, and brown sugar. Using a pastry brush, brush the sauce all over the duck, including inside the cavity.

LET the sauce dry for 15 minutes, then brush again. Repeat until you are left with about 5 tablespoons sauce. Refrigerate the duck uncovered for at least 8 hours or overnight.

PREHEAT the oven to 350°F.

PLACE the duck on a baking rack set inside a roasting pan. Brush the underside of the duck with half of the remaining sauce and roast for 45 minutes. Flip the duck over and brush with the remaining sauce. Roast for another 45 minutes until internal temperature reads 165°F. Remove from the oven and let cool.

SERVE with julienned scallions, mantao (page 19), and hoisin on the side for dipping.

THE PORCELAIN POWER BROKER: MEI LUM OF WING ON WO

When I first walked into Wing on Wo, I was like whoa, where am I? Time warp? Film set? Heaven? Coming from a place as cinematic as Nom Wah, it takes a lot to get that reaction from me. But this 130-year-old institution around the corner on Mott Street is truly transportive. Wing on Wo was one of the first porcelain stores in Chinatown, and now one of the last. To push open the creaky red-framed door, with its melancholy jingle, is to touch Chinatown's living history, a history that is made up of twined links of family. The entire narrow storefront is lined with shelves, and on the shelves rests the most beautiful porcelain I've ever seen: intricately painted plates in crimson and gold, vases featuring complex geometric patterns, tureens that are dead ringers for cabbage. (This is, I learned, the famous cabbage ware.) To the right is a long wooden counter that bears smaller porcelain items like jewelry boxes and chopstick holders, except for an area covered in sheets of the South China Morning Post newspaper, used for wrapping the delicate purchases. And behind the counter are the most precious items: some of the finest hand-painted porcelain teacups, a few pieces from the early days, and an old cash register behind which I first met Mei Lum, the fifth-generation owner of Wing on Wo.

For my money, Lum, age thirty, is one of the most trenchant voices in Chinatown today. After graduating with a degree in East Asian Studies from Mount Holyoke College and spending years in Southeast Asia and China at various nonprofit organizations, Mei returned to New York in 2015 to take over the business at a moment when Wing on Wo could have easily disappeared. She brought with her not just her memories of what the business meant for her family and for her community but the conviction that Wing on Wo could also help redefine what it meant to be a family business in Chinatown in the twenty-first century. Today at Wing on Wo, you're likely to find three generations: Mei up front; her father, Gary, beside her at the register; her grandma Nancy, who ran the business for fifty years; and Nancy's sister, Betty, "Wing on Wo's number one employee," sitting on chairs across from them. Alongside the traditional porcelain, you'll also find collaborations with contemporary artists like zines produced by Asian American artists and capsule collections from up-and-coming porcelain artisans. At night, Mei often hosts talks, screenings, readings, and panels as part of the W.O.W. Project, a community-based organization she founded in 2016. For me, Wing on Wo isn't just an institution of the past but a glimpse of the future as well.

hen my great-great-grandfather Walter Foonpoo immigrated to New York from Toishan in 1890, he found a small community, a few thousand men living around Pell, Doyers, and Mott Streets. Due to the disgraceful Pace Act of 1875, which barred single Chinese women from immigrating to the United States, and the reprehensible Chinese Exclusion Act of 1882, which barred nearly all Chinese immigration, Chinatown was a community full of bachelors.

Some of the the early Chinatown residents had come, like my grandfather, directly from China; many had fled the anti-Chinese persecution on the West Coast. Like most immigrants, especially those who faced discrimination, these men relied on one another for support. My great-great-grandfather founded Wing on Wo as part haven and part home-away-from-home. The store began not as a porcelain shop but as a general store where recent immigrants could purchase different tastes of home—dried herbs, canned goods, salted fish. It was an informal post office, collecting letters hand-carried by recent arrivals bearing news of life back home. They even made their own roast pig and roast chicken in a fire pit in the back, which they served up as a weekend special.

For nearly ninety-five years, Wing on Wo served as a lifeline for the community as my own family grew roots, both in the store and in the country. My great-great-grandfather passed the store to his son, Walter Eng, who ran it in much the same manner as his father had: as a gathering place that also did a brisk business in nearly everything. Then in the early 1960s, two things happened that profoundly changed both the course of Wing on Wo and the Chinese community at large. First, the Chinese Exclusion Act was functionally repealed with the Hart-Celler Act, allowing for the reuniting of families and children and the arrival of Chinese women, a much-needed salve for the loneliness of Chinatown's bachelors. My father, Gary, who was nine years old at the time, remembers that time fondly. "It was so romantic," he says, "there were family celebrations everywhere you turned."

That same year, my great-grandfather, my grandmother's father, suffered a heart attack and passed away, right in this store. He was sixty-nine years old.

With the arrival of entire Chinese families, the desperate need for gathering places like Wing on Wo softened. Happily for our community, now there were families to return home to. With the passing of my great-grandfather, Wing on Wo ventured into new territory. His son and two daughters (my kau gong, my ji po, and my po po) had grown up in the store. My po po, my grandmother Nancy, remembers the clack of mahjong tiles and the smell of roasted pig. For her, as it is for me, Wing on Wo was the backdrop of her childhood, a place she visited to spend time with her father and where she worked after school and on the weekends.

With the passing of Walter, my grandmother, her sister, and her brother took over as best they could. They were committed to keeping the doors open, but neither could do it full-time. My grandmother, thirty-four at the time, was working as a secretary to the commissioner at the Department of Health, where my grandfather Shuck Seid was also working. They met in the neighborhood in 1946

when my grandmother was just sixteen years old. My kau gong, my grand-uncle who worked nights at the post office, would open the store from 2 p.m. to 6 p.m., when he went to work. Then my po po would take over from 6 p.m. to 10 p.m. She was also juggling having three small children at home, including my mom.

My grandmother is, above all, a practical woman, and it didn't take long for her to tire of the general nature of the general store. She didn't want to deal with pigs or chickens. "I wasn't going to cut meat," she often says plainly. Of all the general goods Wing on Wo sold, porcelain stood out to my grandmother for its beauty. So she and my grandfather, who apart from working at the Department of Health worked as commanding officer of the auxiliary police unit at NYPD's 5th Precinct, began traveling back to Hong Kong, visiting porcelain showrooms and shipping back crates and crates of delicate hand-painted vases, bowls, teapots, and teacups. It was then that Wing on Wo took on its character as a porcelain shop.

The golden years spanned the 1970s and 1980s and coincided with the opening of China to Western eyes. After the trade embargo was lifted in 1971 and a trade agreement was reached in 1979, Bloomingdale's held a chain-wide celebration of Chinese textiles, home goods, and porcelain. For many Americans, this was their first exposure to China's rich porcelain tradition. My father calls it China's coming-out party. And that interest trickled down to us. We sold everything from day dinnerware to intricate ivory jewelry.

This was the Wing on Wo I remember as a child. I grew up around the corner in the Chatham Green apartments and I spent a lot of time in the back of the shop, where I shared countless dinners with my family, where I had daily Chinese lessons with my grandfather in the office, and where the stacks and stacks of porcelain imported from Hong Kong were stored. There was a steady stream of neighborhood visitors who didn't come to buy as much as to say hello to ah sim, ah sook (Cantonese for "aunt" and "uncle").

My grandfather was incredibly proud of his heritage and was deeply devoted to the community. In 1975 he established the Chinatown Project, a civilian group of Chinese-speaking interpreters within the NYPD meant to encourage the local community to report crimes. He was the chairman of the Louie Association and was heavily involved in community affairs. Everywhere he went in Chinatown, he was greeted. When my parents were at work—my father, Gary, Wing on Wo's shopkeeper, and my mother, Lorraine, a technical clothing designer—my grandfather would sit with me, teaching me Cantonese poetry while my grandmother made me snacks in the kitchen. We'd gather in the back with my cousins, aunts, and uncles for family dinner almost every night.

My mom and dad met as kids on the Jersey Shore, where both their families had houses, and they married in 1980. My mom is one of three: she has an older sister, Sylven, and had an older brother, Stuart, my uncle Doy Q. My grandparents' idea was that Doy Q would take over the business one day.

As it was for many other businesses in Chinatown, 9/11 was a catastrophe for us. And as for many other families, it was personally devastating. Doy Q, my uncle and my grandparents' only son, worked as the managing director at Sandler O'Neill and Partners and wasn't fortunate enough to evacuate the South Tower. My grandparents, who had been readying themselves to retire, were not only heartbroken, as we all were, but were uncertain about the future of Wing on Wo.

On top of the personal catastrophe of losing Doy Q, 9/11 was a disaster for all of Chinatown's business owners. Chinatown is a stone's throw from the Financial District, and vast swathes of it were shut down for months on end. For small businesses already struggling, as well as factories just coasting on the near side of viability, 9/11 was a cataclysm from which there was no recovery. The garment factories on which much of the local economy depended were immediately frozen. And with it, many of the businesses and restaurants that relied on those workers were impacted too. If my great-grandfather hadn't purchased the building, we'd have gone out of business as well. Those long and dark months turned to years.

The shop grounded my growth in understanding what it meant to be a fourth-generation Chinese American, and at the same time, it also gave me the courage to go beyond the borders of Chinatown. After attending college and working throughout China and Southeast Asia, in 2015, I applied to Columbia University for graduate school and was accepted. I moved back to New York, eager to embark on the next stage of my life. But in the fall of that same year, my dad called me: "Mei," he said, "we're selling the store." I knew things had been difficult,

but it never occurred to me that Wing on Wo would shutter its doors. Now, it seemed that it would soon be on the brink of erasure. My family was already showing it to brokers. I was fortunate enough to have met a PhD student, now professor, Diane Wong, who took me under her wing to deepen my understanding of my relationship with Chinatown. Shadowing conversations with residents, business owners, activists, and property owners about the state of a rapidly changing Chinatown brought me to act quickly and pushed me to decide to step up and take over. My life was shifting, and the life of Wing on Wo would have another chance.

After all, my work community building abroad was exactly the same sort of spirit that would regenerate Wing on Wo. Wing on Wo was a haven, a home-away-from-home for hundreds of immigrants across almost a century. More personally, it was *my* home-away-from-home. With the support of my parents and my grandparents, I stepped into a primary leadership role.

My vision for Wing on Wo has been twofold. On one side is the business. I knew we wouldn't survive if we continued to exclusively sell traditional porcelain as we had since the '60s. My grandparents bought their porcelain from broker showrooms in Hong Kong, where my grandfather had emigrated from at age fourteen. But the majority of porcelain, and certainly the high-end porcelain, originates in Jingdezhen, a city in southeastern China known as the Porcelain Capital. I partnered with Nate Brown, a filmmaker and my best friend who lived in Jingdezhen, to buy directly from artisans. Not only does that allow us to select our own wares directly from the source, but it gives us the opportunity to explore up-and-coming porcelain artists like Dao Jin and Huaya in addition to stocking traditional patterns.

The other side of the business is grounded by our rich, thriving community through a community-based organization that I founded out of the shop in 2016: the W.O.W. Project. The W.O.W. Project creates space for conversations to happen across language barriers, economic backgrounds, and generational gaps to actively shape the future of Chinatown. We host panel discussions, screenings, poetry readings, and much more in the effort to build intergenerational bridges of understanding for Chinatown's beautiful thriving future.

Over my lifetime at Wing on Wo, everything and nothing has changed. Today, I'm behind the register. My grandmother often sits across from me. Her sister, my aunt Betty, is there beside her. My father, now retired, is in the back office or often here by my side. My mom tends to the flowers and plants that line the front window. My cousins—Doy Q's children, Evan and Kara—help out with our Instagram and frequently assist on the weekends. My sister, Lina, lends a hand with strategy and brings me snacks as a pick-me-up during the most stressful times. And though we don't do it every night, you'll likely find us in the back kitchen after the lights go out, sitting down together to enjoy a family dinner.

FROM LEFT TO RIGHT: Garlic Chili Cucumbers (p. 218); Chinese Greens with Oyster Sauce (p. 217)

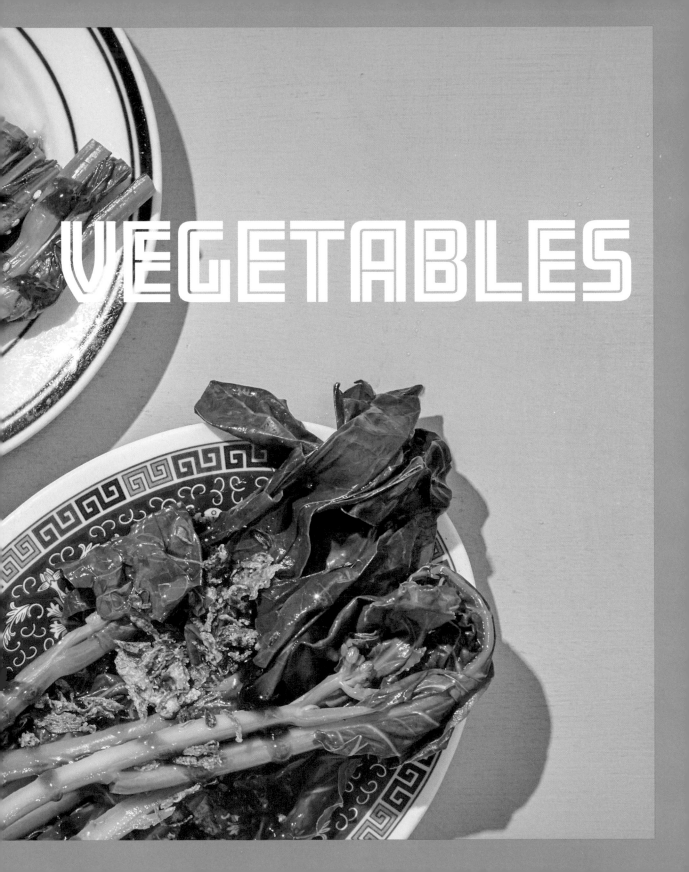

VEGETABLES

Traditionally the working-class Cantonese diet was largely vegetable-based. Thanks to the blessings of poverty! Now, for many of the Chinese immigrants who've made the journey from poor to middle class, meat consumption is a status symbol. Good for esteem; terrible for arteries. Interestingly, at Nom Wah, we get the bulk of our vegan and vegetarian requests from younger non-Chinese clientele. And we're more than happy to accommodate since the dim sum repertoire has its share of veggie-forward (and otherwise green) options. Most Cantonese cooking relies on leafy greens: bok choy, choy sum (Chinese flowering cabbage), and gai lan (Chinese broccoli, which is leafy and much sweeter than Western broccoli). The methods for cooking them are all similar, so just go to the veg aisle and go crazy.

TIGER BEER PICKLES

SERVES 7

I'm pretty sure Calvin came up with this recipe the same way ancient picklers came up with theirs: he looked around to see what he had lying around in the way of brines and poured it on. Cal loves beer. He loves Tiger Beer. Ergo, Tiger Beer pickles. The beer adds sweetness; the vinegar does the chemical work of fermentation; and that sambal oelek adds a kick in the pants of spice.

½ tablespoon toasted sesame seeds
1 tallboy can of Tiger Beer
4 cups distilled white vinegar
2 cups sambal oelek
2 cups sugar
4 cups water
1½ pounds bok choy, quartered
1 medium carrot, shaved on mandoline
8 ounces bean sprouts
6 cloves garlic, thinly sliced

SPREAD sesame seeds on a sheet tray and toast oven at 350°F for 10 minutes or until fragrant.

MEANWHILE. in a large bowl, mix together the beer, vinegar, sambal oelek, sugar, and water until the sugar is dissolved.
PLACE the bok choy, carrot, bean sprouts, and garlic in a 12-quart glass jar. Pour the Tiger Beer pickling liquid over the top, making sure the vegetables are submerged.
COVER, put in a cool dry place, and allow to pickle for at least 48 hours. When serving, garnish with the toasted sesame seeds.

VEGETABLES

CHINESE GREENS WITH OYSTER SAUCE

SERVES 4

2 pounds Chinese broccoli (gai lan) or other leafy greens
2 tablespoons toasted sesame oil
½ cup oyster sauce
Toasted sesame seeds for garnish
Fried shallots for garnish, available at most Asian groceries

IF the Chinese broccoli stalks are large, slice the greens lengthwise from leaf to bottom of stem, as many cuts as necessary to get to an edible size.

BRING a large pot of water to a boil.

MEANWHILE, make an ice bath by filling a bowl three-quarters of the way with half ice and half water. Keep away from the stove so the ice bath doesn't melt.

ONCE the water is boiling, add the greens and cook for 30 seconds to 1 minute, until bright vibrant green. Using tongs, transfer to the ice bath. Let sit for 30 seconds more before draining and transferring to a clean bowl.

DRIZZLE the greens with the toasted sesame oil and oyster sauce and toss to coat. Garnish with toasted sesame seeds and fried shallots and serve.

GARLIC CHILI CUCUMBERS

SERVES 4

These easy-to-make cucumbers have a kick in them and are great for cutting through the fatty richness of dim sum. Use the excess chili sauce to add a kick to any of your other vegetables whenever you wish.

FOR THE GARLIC PASTE:
6 whole cloves garlic, peeled
1½ teaspoons neutral oil

FOR THE CHILI SAUCE:
1½ cups Lao Gan Ma's Spicy Chili Crisp
¾ cup sambal oelek
¾ cup brown sugar
1⅓ cups distilled white vinegar

FOR THE CUCUMBERS:
4 medium Kirby cucumbers
5 tablespoons chili sauce (see above)
1½ tablespoons light soy sauce
1½ tablespoons Dumpling Dipping Sauce (page 35)
1 teaspoon salt

TO MAKE THE GARLIC PASTE:
IN a mini food processor, process the garlic and neutral oil until pureed.

TO MAKE THE CHILI SAUCE:
IN a large bowl, combine all the ingredients and mix well.

TO MAKE THE CUCUMBERS:
CUT the tips off the cucumbers. Halve them lengthwise, then quarter them and cut the quarters on an extreme bias into 1-inch-thick pieces.
TOSS cucumbers with 1½ teaspoons of the garlic paste, the chili sauce, the Dumpling Dipping Sauce, and the salt. Cover and refrigerate for 3 to 4 hours before serving.

CLOCKWISE FROM TOP: Steamed Red Bean Buns (p. 232);
Steamed Phoenix Buns (p. 233); Steamed Lotus Seed Buns (p. 232);
Fried Sesame Balls with Lotus Paste (p. 223)

DESSERTS

The traditional American meal often ends with a carboholic train wreck called dessert: when all the prudence exhibited earlier on in the day is abandoned for an orgy of sugar, chocolate, and cream. Not so in dim sum. The reasons for this include a) common sense and b) the fact that dim sum was meant to be a fast meal in the morning when no one is going to take the time for an extra course. Also the traditional Southern Chinese palate isn't keen for the saccharine, nor are the Chinese sweet on chocolate. A recent study showed that the Chinese eat on average less than one bar per capita every year.

At most dim sum parlors, it's a chicken-and-egg thing. We are surrounded by a slew of dessert-focused businesses, from the ice cream and egg waffles at Eggloo to the sponge cakes of Kam Hing Coffee Shop. Did they pop up because dessert is so overlooked on most dim sum menus or are dim sum menus light on dessert because they offer alternatives? But at Nom Wah, dessert is part of our DNA. After all, Uncle Wally rose through the ranks for his proficiency at moon cakes, and for years, we survived almost exclusively on our red bean and lotus pastes. So though not the shimmering patisserie you might find at Dominique Ansel's or the sprinkle-and-chocolate cookies of Veniero's or extravagant cakes of Lady M's, Nom Wah's desserts are not to be missed. They aren't an afterthought. They're an afterword.

FRIED SESAME BALLS WITH LOTUS PASTE

MAKES 20 SESAME BALLS

Basically delicious Chinese profiteroles, jin deui, or sesame balls, are made with glutinous rice, which gives the dough that yielding, slightly gooey texture. This is the perfect foil for the crunch of the sesame seed carapace and the inner payload of sweetened lotus paste (made with lotus seeds, easily gotten at any Asian grocery store.) Well, traditionally it's lotus paste, and that's what we still use, but that's the thing about an empty ball: you can fill it with what you like.

FOR THE LOTUS PASTE:
½ cup dried lotus seeds
⅓ cup sugar
⅛ teaspoon salt
1½ tablespoons lard (can substitute shortening or neutral oil)

FOR THE SESAME BALLS:
½ cup plus 1 tablespoon sugar
4½ cups glutinous rice flour
¼ cup lotus seed paste (see above)
⅛ cup sesame seeds
Neutral oil, to fry

TO MAKE THE LOTUS PASTE:

PLACE the lotus seeds into a pot with enough water to submerge the seeds twice over. Bring to a simmer over medium-low heat, cover, and simmer for 1 hour, or until the seeds are easily mashed with a fork.

USING a slotted spoon, remove the seeds and drain off any excess liquid. Add to a food processor with 2 tablespoons water and process until a loose, pastelike texture forms. Add additional water, 1 tablespoon at a time, if the mixture seems too thick or chalky.

TRANSFER the paste to a large skillet along with the sugar and salt and cook over low heat, stirring continuously to avoid sticking. When the paste becomes slightly firmer, after about 20 minutes, turn off the heat and fold in the lard. The end product should be shiny, have a texture close to cookie dough, and stick to the spoon. Set aside to cool.

TO MAKE THE SESAME BALLS:

IN a small pan, bring 3 cups of water to a boil. Stir in the sugar until it dissolves and forms a smooth syrup.

IN a large bowl, combine the glutinous rice flour and syrup and knead into a dough.

PLACE half the dough in a large, heavy-bottomed pot and cook over medium heat for 1 minute, or until it starts to become translucent. Add the cooked dough to the raw dough and knead together on a lightly floured surface until fully incorporated, approximately 3 minutes.

DIVIDE the dough into roughly 1-inch-diameter balls.

SLIGHTLY flatten each piece of dough, put about 1 teaspoon of lotus seed paste in the middle, and close up the ball, rolling it gently between your palms.

FILL a small bowl with cold water and quickly dip each ball in the water before rolling in sesame seeds to coat.

FILL a large pot with enough oil to submerge the balls and heat to 350ºF over medium-high heat.

ADD the sesame balls, working in batches if needed, and fry until they're golden brown all over and float to the top of the oil. Using a spider, carefully remove balls and set aside on a paper towel–lined plate to drain before serving.

ALMOND COOKIES

MAKES 18 COOKIES

When I was a kid, Uncle Wally used to sneak me freshly baked almond cookies when we visited Nom Wah. Even when they're just out of the oven, these classic Guangdong treats crumble easily. They all but disappear when dipped into a cup of tea. Years later, when I first heard the expression "That's the way the cookie crumbles," I was confused, since I grew up associating cookies crumbling with the secret joys of Saturday visits to Uncle Wally's. Today, this is one of the few survivors of our days as a bakery, but I keep it on the menu hoping that some future Wilson Tang is forming sweet almond cookie memories at this very moment.

1¼ cups all-purpose flour
¾ cup powdered sugar
3 tablespoons cornstarch
1 teaspoon baking soda
1 teaspoon baking powder
3 egg yolks (place 2 in one bowl and 1 in another bowl)
½ cup melted lard, cooled to room temperature
1 teaspoon almond extract
18 raw almonds

SIFT the flour, powdered sugar, cornstarch, baking soda, and baking powder into a large bowl. Sift together once more, into another bowl, to make sure the ingredients are well incorporated.

ADD the lard to the bowl of 2 egg yolks and beat until combined. Add the almond extract and stir to combine. Using a rubber spatula, fold this mixture into the dry ingredients, then knead with your hands for 3 to 5 minutes to create a dough ball. Don't overwork the dough or the cookie will lose its flaky texture. Cover and allow the dough to rest for 20 minutes.

MEANWHILE, preheat the oven to 350°F.

SPREAD the almonds on a baking sheet and toast for 5 minutes.

BEAT the remaining egg yolk and set aside.

DIVIDE the dough into 18 equal pieces. Roll each piece into a golf ball–sized ball and transfer to a baking sheet, spacing them at least 2 inches apart.

BRUSH all sides of the dough balls with beaten egg yolk and let sit for 1 minute. Then brush them once more. Press 1 toasted almond onto the center of each dough ball. Bake for 15 to 18 minutes, until golden. Remove, let cool for 15 minutes on a baking tray, then serve.

MOON CAKES

MAKES ABOUT 24 MOON CAKES

Moon cakes, or jyut beng, are part of Nom Wah's DNA. Excellence in moon cake–making, gleaned in Hong Kong, is what kept Uncle Wally on and helped him move up with the Choys, Nom Wah's former owners, when he first arrived. It's what kept the bakery going in those long, quiet years when it was more a social club than business concern. Wally's red bean paste—a common moon cake filling—is literally our lifeblood. And yet today we no longer make moon cakes. As the business changed from retail to wholesale and back to retail; as we focused more on savory dim sum, moving away from our original bakery days; as other bakeries have opened specializing in these delicate pastries—shells pressed into molds, insides filled with everything from red bean paste to cured duck eggs and served during the Mid-Autumn Festival—we stopped our own production. And yet I'm not sad about it in the least.

Look, dim sum wasn't ever going anywhere, but that it would flourish was no certain thing. That there would be young Chinese Americans who'd pick up the mantle of what dim sum could be in the United States and build their lives around that promise wasn't assured. And yet . . . and yet recently I met a guy named Guorang Fan. Fan, as he's called, is a handsome thirty-two-year-old kid from Brooklyn who, after a career in e-commerce, decided to get seriously into the dim sum game. Fan, who worked at the legendary Tim Ho Wan, runs a place down in Jacksonville, Florida, called Tim Wah Dim Sum. "I am the Chinese community," he likes to joke. I first met him on Instagram, where I meet everybody these days, when he slid into my DMs. I checked out his feed, which consists either of videos of him doing muscle-ups (he's very strong) or the most beautiful dumplings and moon cakes I've ever seen. What follows is Fan's recipe, and it gives me great joy that people like Fan are out there, people with the hustle and passion to carry on these ancient traditions for a new era.

4¼ cups pastry flour

⅖ cup peanut oil

1⅓ cups Lyle's Golden Syrup

1½ tablespoons kansui (alkaline water; you can buy it at any Asian grocery store—we recommend Koon Chun brand)

1 recipe red bean paste (page 232) or lotus paste (page 223)

1 large egg, beaten

SPECIAL EQUIPMENT:

Moon cake mold (available on Amazon)

IN a large bowl, mix together the flour, peanut oil, syrup, and kansui. Knead until a smooth, stiff dough forms, 5 to 10 minutes. Let rest, covered, for 30 minutes.

AFTER the dough is rested, divide it into about 24 Ping-Pong-sized balls (about 10 grams each). Dusting with pastry flour as needed to prevent sticking, flatten them out using a rolling pin or a tortilla press until ⅛ inch thick (about the thickness of a dumpling wrapper).

PLACE a teaspoon-sized ball of bean paste in the center of each wrapper. Pinch the dough around it to close the cake, rolling it loosely between your palms to make a smooth sphere. Just make sure not to have too much dough at the seams.

PLACE each sphere into the moon cake press. If it sticks, dust a little pastry flour on the press.

PREHEAT the oven to 425°F and line a baking sheet with parchment paper. Place the moon cakes on the prepared baking sheet, leaving about 1 inch between them.

SPRAY a little water on top of each moon cake, then bake them in the oven for 5 minutes, or until they develop a faint yellowish color. Remove from the oven and brush the tops with the beaten egg.

REDUCE the oven temperature to 350°F. Return the moon cakes to the oven and bake for 10 to 12 minutes, until golden brown, rotating the pan 5 minutes through so they bake evenly. Remove from oven and let cool completely. Serve immediately or store in an airtight container for up to a week.

STEAMED DESSERT BUNS

There's a tremendous symmetry to dim sum feasts: you start with a steamed bun filled with char siu, and you end with a steamed bun filled with lotus, red bean, or custard. From the outside, these buns look identical—they use the same dough recipe—but inside each bursts with its own character. As a kid—forced to sit through endless hours of Chinese school, pressured into living up to the ideal of the model minority—I always found this fact strangely moving. Among my favorites is the phoenix bun, with a custard filling made with an abundance of egg yolks. Underneath an obedient exterior, there's some wild shit going on.

STEAMED LOTUS SEED BUNS

MAKES 10 BUNS

1 recipe Basic Bao Dough (page 16)
1 recipe lotus paste (see page 223)

TO assemble, place 2 tablespoons of filling in each bao and prepare according to the instructions for making bao (see page 17).

STEAMED RED BEAN BUNS

MAKES 10 BUNS

1 pound dried red (adzuki) beans
3½ cups water
¼ cup neutral oil
1 cup brown sugar
1 recipe Basic Bao Dough (page 16)

RINSE the adzuki beans and drain. Put them in a large pot and add the water. Cover and bring to a boil. Reduce heat to simmer and cook, stirring occasionally, until soft, 1½ to 2 hours.

DRAIN the beans, transfer to a food processor, and process into a puree.
IN a large nonstick skillet, heat the neutral oil over medium-low heat. Add the puree and brown sugar and cook, stirring frequently, until a thick paste forms, 30 to 40 minutes. Transfer to a bowl and let cool before using. You can refrigerate the filling for up to 24 hours before using.
TO assemble, place 2 tablespoons of filling in each bao and prepare according to the instructions for making bao (see page 17).

STEAMED PHOENIX BUNS

MAKES 6 BUNS

FOR THE FILLING:

1 egg yolk

2 salted egg yolks (buy salted duck eggs
and discard the whites)

3½ tablespoons unsalted butter, at room
temperature

1½ tablespoon sugar

1½ tablespoons custard powder

1½ tablespoons milk powder

FOR THE DOUGH:

1⅔ cups all-purpose flour

5 teaspoons sugar

1 teaspoon active dry yeast

1⅛ teaspoons neutral oil

½ cup plus 1½ teaspoons whole milk

TO MAKE THE FILLING:

PREPARE a steamer according to the
instructions on page 10. Carefully slip the
egg yolk into a heatproof bowl, add the salted
egg yolks, and steam for 12 minutes until
solid. Carefully remove the bowl and mash
the yolks together until crumbly.

IN a separate bowl, mash the butter flat with
a rubber spatula. Fold the sugar into the
butter. Sift the custard powder and milk
powder into the butter-and-sugar mixture
and stir to combine. Add the mashed-up
yolks and mix thoroughly. Wrap the filling in
plastic wrap and refrigerate for 3 hours.

AFTER 3 hours, divide the filling into 6 equal-
sized pieces of about 20 grams (¾ ounce)
each. Roll each piece into a ball and place

them on a plate, covered, in the refrigerator
for 1 hour.

TO MAKE THE DOUGH AND ASSEMBLE:

IN a large bowl, combine the flour, sugar,
yeast, and neutral oil and stir together with a
pair of chopsticks.

ADD about half of the milk into the mixture.
Mix thoroughly, add the remaining milk,
and mix again. Use your hands to bring the
mixture together into a sticky ball of dough.
Turn the dough onto a work surface and
continue kneading for about 10 minutes,
until it is pliable and no longer sticky.

DIVIDE the dough into 6 equal-sized pieces
and shape them into balls. Cover with plastic
wrap after each is made.

TO form your buns, flatten the balls of dough
so that the sides are a bit thinner than the
centers. This helps prevent the filling from
bursting out when steaming.

PLACE a piece of filling into the center of the
dough and pinch the dough closed around
it, rolling it loosely in your palms to form
a smooth ball. Let the buns sit at room
temperature for 35 minutes.

PREPARE a steamer. Add the buns and steam
for 10 minutes until firm with a bit of give,
leaving the lid ajar just slightly. This will help
keep the filling runny rather than custardy.
Turn off the heat and let the buns sit for 3
minutes before serving.

CLOCKWISE FROM LEFT: Steamed Phoenix Buns (p. 233); Fried Sesame Balls with Lotus Paste (p. 223); Steamed Lotus Seed Buns (p. 232)

LUNAR NEW YEAR

t was overcast on January 25, Lunar New Year, and rain came unexpectedly. The clouds cast a pall on this, the most important holiday for us, but they weren't the only gloomy harbinger. The night before a fire had ripped through the archives of the Museum of Chinese in America, not the fancy building on Centre Street but the original location on Mulberry Street. Technically, the fire started a few floors above, but in the deluge of FDNY hoses, the archives were all but assuredly destroyed. I had been there a few weeks before, to chat with the assistant director of collections Kevin Chu and had admired the boxes and boxes of private archives he had shown me. Each was neatly labeled with the name of the family who had donated their most cherished keepsakes. I wonder where all those keepsakes are now. What's more, the coronavirus, a scary, tragic, and deadly illness, had just begun to make headlines here in America. The Chinese community was terrified, the Chinese American community too, and we all were uncertain of what the future might hold for us. Apart from the clear worry about the health of not only our compatriots and loved ones but all those who might be affected, we were also wary of any backlash we might face as Chinese Americans. Would our businesses suffer? Would we be stigmatized?

Finally, we had a plumbing issue late the night before, and I had been up until 3 or 4 a.m. dealing with contractors trying to make sure we'd be open in the morning. The issue was fixed, but I was almost delirious with exhaustion.

It was under this gray sky and among these dark thoughts that I turned the corner of Doyers Street a few minutes before opening time to see Nom Wah. What a surprise. Before our doors stood a mass of maybe twenty-five or thirty people—umbrellas out, jackets zipped—eagerly waiting to get in. I reached the front door, where my cousin Vincent unlocked it, feeling a bit like a groupie heading backstage at a rock concert. Except this was my concert. Or, it was *our* concert. Inside, the staff, many of whom had been there since 5 a.m., were preparing for the day. The tea had been brewed. The dumplings had been made. The bao was ready for steaming.

An hour or so after opening, the insistent beat of a drum and clash of cymbals announced the arrival of the lion dancers from the Choy Lay Fut Lion and Dance Team. Louder, louder, louder the sound became until the company arrived at our doorway. A crowd had formed, made up of onlookers, those already eating who had rushed outside, and those waiting to be seated. The dragons were bright and colorful, as usual, but their heads were wrapped in plastic wrap to protect them from the rain. Underneath and around them, a dozen young Chinese men and women, members of the troupe, wore black outfits, clapped cymbals, and took turns as the undulating body of the two dragons. I was offered a long red pole with a head of lettuce attached to it. According to custom, I knew the dragon would theatrically leap up to grab the vegetable, devouring it with abandon. This would confer good luck for the upcoming year.

Amid the clamor and clanging, a million thoughts ran through my mind. Some were the worries of a business owner, especially one of a hundred-year-old business in a hundred-year-old building. Some were a more disparate anxiety, an uncertainty as to what the future held, and some were straight-up heartbreak—the smoke could still be seen from the museum fire. But as the lions danced, other thoughts entered my mind too. The hundred years we had survived already. The hundreds of lives Nom Wah has already touched, both among our staff and our customers. Wun Gaw. The twenty cooks busy in the kitchen. My cousin Vincent. Calvin. Julie. The sense of deep community support I feel on a day-to-day basis from my Chinatown brethren whose stories are similar to mine in some ways and still completely their own: of Nancy and Joanne, Mei and Freeman, Paul and Tim and Sophia. I thought of this past decade, how each Lunar New Year I hold this pole but how for the ninety years before that, it was held by someone else, Uncle Wally probably, the Choys before, and that though colorful lion puppets are remade every year and the dancers grow out of dancing, the dance remains as vibrant as ever.

After a few minutes of waving the lettuce, the moment had come. One dancer, holding the head, leaped upon the shoulders of the other. The lion reared its head and opened its mouth. A hand emerged to grab the lettuce, tear it up, and spit it back out. Another troupe member fired a tube of confetti into the sky. I looked up as bright squares of crepe paper—pink, red, yellow, purple, white, gold, and silver—filled the sky. Color against the gray, fragile perhaps and fleeting but nevertheless here.

ACKNOWLEDGMENTS

FROM WILSON TANG:

This book belongs not just to me but to the hundreds of Nom Wah employees over the last one hundred years. Without them, this book wouldn't exist. I'd also like to thank the following:

Barb Leung, for pushing me to pursue this project and making sure it came to fruition; Joshua David Stein, for writing the damn thing; Eric Li, for his generosity and expertise and making Nom Wah Philly a success; Zhiyu Lai, for opening up our fast-casual outposts with me. A big shout-out to Julie Cole at Nom Wah Nolita and Wun Gaw at Nom Wah OG, both of whom provided the recipes for this volume and keep the Nom Wah empire well supplied with dim sum. I'd like to thank Vincent Tang and his father, Fred, who have provided support both publicly and privately; Calvin Eng, who opened Nolita and is still—and will always be—fam. Uncle Wally, for carrying Nom Wah and all it represents on his shoulders for decades. My mom and dad, for carrying me on their shoulders and later putting up with me. My wife, Mae, for currently putting up with me. Ditto my kids, Ryan and Lucy, who never once complained that Dad was always off shouting into a phone. Guorong Fan,

master of moon cakes and muscle-ups. All the contributors in this book: Joanne Kwong, Mei Lum, Nancy Yao Maasbach, Freeman Wong, Paul Eng, Sophia Ng Tsao. The team at Ecco: Dan Halpern, Sara Birmingham, Renata de Oliveira. The early and continued supporters of Nom Wah, including Gretchen Viehmann, Andrew Zimmern, and Alex Guarnaschelli. Alex Lau, Elizabeth Jaime, Sue Li, Shauna Candella, and An Rong Xu, for making dim sum sexy. Sarah Zorn, for

making sure dim sum is functional. Maral Varolian, for her beautiful illustrations, and Rica Allannic, my agent, for being a shrewd, supportive, and effective book doula.

FROM JOSHUA DAVID STEIN:

First of all, I want to thank Wilson for entrusting me to help tell the story of Nom Wah Tea Parlor, to which I've been going since I moved to New York twenty years ago. I always arrived hungry and I always left satisfied. This project is no different.

This book also wouldn't have been possible without the tireless and somewhat frightening assistance of Barb Leung, who made sure the many moving parts lined up. So Barb, thank you. Vincent Tang, the Wun Gaw whisperer, thank you for overcoming your fear of Wun Gaw, and Wun Gaw, thank you for letting me into your kitchen and for the literally thousands of dumplings I've eaten during the course of this book. Julie Cole was and is a generous soul, giving recipes, time, and an immense care above and beyond her duty, and Calvin Eng, who doesn't even work at Nom Wah anymore

and technically has no duties to go beyond but also went beyond his for reasons I'm still not sure of. O Alex Lau, powerful man, lens wonder, street wanderer, image capturer. It was a pleasure shooting with you.

In addition, as this project concerned not just Wilson and the Nom Wah family but others in the community, I specifically want to thank Mei Lum, Timothy Hsu, Freeman Wong, Nancy Yao Maasbach, Kevin Chu, Joanne Kwong, Sophia Ng Tsao, and Paul Eng. Karen Zhou, executive director of Homecrest Community Services, was immensely helpful arranging and later translating my interviews with Wally Tang. I want to express my gratitude to Wally Tang, shy at first, for trusting a stranger enough to share your life.

Finally, thank you to Sara Birmingham, our stellar editor at Ecco, as well as Sarah Zorn, our lifesaving recipe tester, Sarah Smith, my agent on this project at David Black, and the honorary Sarah, Rica Allannic, without whom this project never would have happened.

INDEX

(Page references in *italics* refer to illustrations.)

A

Adidas, 15, 54, 58
aji-mirin, 4
Almond Cookies, *226,* 227
Aqua Best, New York, 102–7, *103, 105, 106*
Arancini, Egg Fried Rice, with Sambal Kewpie,
    164–65, *165*

B

Bacon and Shrimp Balls, *156–57,* 160
balls, 156–65, *159*
    Egg Fried Rice Arancini with Sambal
        Kewpie, 164–65, *165*
    Fried Shrimp Crab Claw, *162,* 163
    Shrimp, *156–57,* 160–63, *161*
    Shrimp and Bacon, *156–57,* 160, *161*
bamboo shoots:
    No Pork No Shrimp Master Filling, 43
    Vegetable Bao, *12,* 22–23
bao, 9, 12–23
    Dough, Basic, 16–17
    House Special Roast Pork Buns (Char Siu
        Bao), *13, 20, 21*
    how to stuff and close, 17
    Mantao, *12, 14, 18, 19*
    Shanghainese Soup Dumplings (Xiao Long
        Bao), 70–72, *71*
    Vegetable, *12,* 22–23
    see also steamed dessert buns
bean curd, dried (also called tofu skin):
    making, 93

    Vegetable Bao, 22–23
Bean Curd Skin Rolls, Steamed, 93–95, *94*
    Chinese Gravy for, 95
    Shrimp, *94,* 95, *162*
    Vegetable, 95
beef:
    Filet, Cantonese-Style, *196,* 197
    Triple C (Chinese Chopped Cheese)
        Dumplings, *52,* 58–59
black beans, fermented, 3–4
black mushrooms, *see* shiitake mushrooms
bok choy, in Tiger Beer Pickles, 215
"breath of wok," 11
broccoli, Chinese (gai lan):
    Chinese Greens with Oyster Sauce, *212–13,*
        216, 217
    Vegetable Bao, *12,* 22–23
Broth, Vegetarian, 51
buns, *see* bao; steamed dessert buns

C

cabbage:
    and Chicken Dumplings, Pan-Fried, 46,
        47
    No Pork No Shrimp Master Filling, 43
cakes, *108–9,* 110–17, *111*
    Scallion Pancakes, 112–13
    Taro Hash, *116,* 117
    Turnip, 114–15, *115*
Canal Street Market, New York, 80, 84
Cantonese diet, vegetables vs. meat in, 22, 214

Cantonese-style:
    Beef Filet, *196, 197*
    Taro and Pork Belly Casserole, 198, *199*
    see also rice noodle rolls, Cantonese-style
        (cheung fun)
Chaoshan teas, 81
char siu:
    Bao (House Special Roast Pork Buns), *13,*
        20, 21
    Family Meal, *182,* 183
    Noodles, *142,* 143
Cheese, Triple C (Chinese Chopped Cheese)
    Dumplings, *52,* 58–59
chef's specials, 168–83
    Char Siu Family Meal, *182,* 183
    Chicken Feet, 171–72, *173*
    Eggplant, Stuffed, *174, 175*
    Pork Chops, Salt-and-Pepper (and Its Friend
        Sweet-and-Sour Pork Chops), *168, 177,*
        178–79
    Shrimp, Salt-and-Pepper, *169,* 176, *177*
    Spareribs, Steamed, 180, *181*
Chen family (Pearl River Mart), 120–25
cheung fun, *see* rice noodle rolls, Cantonese-style
chicken:
    and Cabbage Dumplings, Pan-Fried, 46, *47*
    Egg Rolls, OG, 99–100, *101*
    Feet, 171–72, *173*
    powder, 3
    Siu Mai, 63, *64*
    Sloppy Joe Noodles (aka Spicy Chicken
        Bolognese Served over Wheat
        Noodles), 146–47
chili:
    Garlic Cucumbers, 218, *219*
    oil, 6
    pickled red, 6
    Sauce, 218
Chimichurri Sauce, Dill, 58–59
Chinatown Project, 209

Chinese Exclusion Act (1882), ix–x, 206
Chive and Shrimp Har Gow, *30–31,* 69, *69*
Chop Suey (Coe), 99
Chorizo Potato Dumplings with Dill Chimichurri
    Sauce, *53,* 56–57
Choy, Ed and May, ix–x, 27–28
Cilantro and Scallion Rice Rolls, *82–83,* 89
cleavers, Chinese, 2–3
Coe, Andrew, 99
Cole, Julie, xv, 22, 49, 144, 164, 202
Cookies, Almond, *226,* 227
cornstarch, 5
cotton kitchen towels, 2
Crab Claw Balls, Fried Shrimp, *162,* 163
Cucumbers, Garlic Chili, 218, *219*
cuttlefish, in Shrimp Master Filling, 42

D

daikon (Chinese radishes), in Turnip Cakes,
    114–15, *115*
desserts, 220–35
    Almond Cookies, *226,* 227
    Moon Cakes, 228–30, *229*
    Sesame Balls, Fried, with Lotus Paste,
        223–24, *225, 234–35*
    see also steamed dessert buns
Dill Chimichurri Sauce, 58–59
dim sum, 6–11
    big three techniques for, 10–11
    fillings vs. wrappers in, 7–9
    in Hong Kong, 26
    origin and early history of, xiv–xv, 14, 80
dipping sauces:
    Dumpling, 39
    Sweet, 87
Duck, Peking, *190, 202, 203*
Dumpling Dipping Sauce, 35
dumplings, 9, 30–75
    automatic dumpling-wrapping machine for,
        66

Chicken and Cabbage, Pan-Fried, 46, *47*

Chicken Siu Mai, 63, *64*

Chorizo Potato, with Dill Chimichurri Sauce, *53,* 56–57

Edamame, *48,* 49–50

Edamame, in Soup, 51, *51*

fillings vs. wrappers, 7–9

Fried Wu Gok, 73–74, *75*

gauu zi, about, 33, 37–39

Har Gow, *30–31, 33,* 66–69, *67, 69*

how to make, 33–35, 38–39

No Pork No Shrimp Master Filling for, 43

pan-frying after steaming, 11

Pork, Pan-Fried, House Special, *30–31, 44,* 45

Pork Master Filling for, 41

Pork Siu Mai, *64,* 65

Shrimp and Chive Har Gow, *30–31,* 69, *69*

Shrimp and Snow Pea Leaf Har Gow, *30–31,* 69, *69*

Shrimp Master Filling for, 42

Shrimp Siu Mai, *64,* 65

siu mai, about, 33, 60–62

Soup, Shanghainese (Xiao Long Bao), 70–72, *71*

Sweet Potato Kale Wontons, *52–53,* 54–55

Triple C (Chinese Chopped Cheese), *52,* 58–59

types of, 33

dumpling skins:

    preferred brand of, 33

    store-bought vs. homemade, 33

E

Edamame Dumplings, *48,* 49–50

    in Soup, 51, *51*

egg:

    Fried Rice, 129

    Fried Rice Arancini with Sambal Kewpie, 164–65, *165*

Rolls, OG, 99–100, *101*

    and Shrimp Fried Rice, *127, 128,* 129

eggplant:

    Garlic, Noodles, *138, 144, 145*

    Stuffed, *174,* 175

Eng, Calvin, 40, 54, 56, 58, 117, 215, 240

Eng, Paul, 184–89, *185*

equipment, 1–3

Essex Pearl, New York, 107

F

Family Meal, Char Siu, *182,* 183

feasts, 190–203

    Beef Filet, Cantonese-Style, *196,* 197

    Duck, Peking, *190,* 202, *203*

    Shiitake Mushrooms and Lettuce, *200,* 201

    Taro and Pork Belly Casserole, Cantonese-Style, 198, *199*

    Walnut Shrimp, 193–94, *195*

fermented black beans, 3–4

fillings vs. wrappers, 7–9

Fong On, New York, 184–89, *185, 187, 188*

Foonpoo, Walter, 206

Fried Dough (Youtiao), 90, *91*

fried rice, 128

    Egg, 129

    Egg, Arancini with Sambal Kewpie, 164–65, *165*

    Shrimp and Egg, *127, 128,* 129

Fried Sesame Balls with Lotus Paste, 223–24, *225, 234–35*

Fried Wu Gok, 73–74, *75*

Fujian, Fujianese immigrants, xiii, 80, 81, 104

G

garlic:

    Chili Cucumbers, 218, *219*

    Eggplant Noodles, *138, 144, 145*

    fried (jarred), 6

    Paste, 218

gauu zi (dumplings), 33, *36*, 37–59, 60
  Chicken and Cabbage Dumplings, Pan-Fried, 46, *47*
  Chorizo Potato Dumplings with Dill Chimichurri Sauce, *53*, 56–57
  Dumpling Dipping Sauce for, 35
  Edamame Dumplings, *48*, 49–50
  Edamame Dumplings in Soup, 51, *51*
  how to make, 38–39
  pan-frying after steaming, 11
  Pork Dumplings, Pan-Fried, House Special, *30–31*, *44*, 45
  Sweet Potato Kale Wontons, *52–53*, 54–55
  three master fillings for, 7–9, 40–43
  Triple C (Chinese Chopped Cheese) Dumplings, *52*, 58–59
gelatin cubes, making, 70, 72
glutinous rice, or sticky rice (also called sweet rice), 4, 131
  Sticky Rice with Chinese Sausage, *126*, *130*, 131
glutinous rice flour, 5
Gravy, Chinese, for Steamed Bean Curd Rolls, 95
greens, Chinese:
  Ho Fun Noodle Soup with, *148*, 149
  with Oyster Sauce, *212–13*, *216*, 217

H

Hak Box, New York, 84
hardware, 1–3
Har Gow, *30–31*, 33, 66–69, *67*, *69*
  automatic dumpling-wrapping machine for, 66
  Shrimp and Chive, *30–31*, *69*, 69
  Shrimp and Snow Pea Leaf, *30–31*, *69*, 69
Ho Fun Noodle Soup with Chinese Greens, *148*, 149
Hong Kong:
  dim sum kitchens in, 26

flight of Chinese immigrants to, during civil war, 24–26
House Special Pan-Fried Pork Dumplings, *44*, 45
House Special Roast Pork Buns (Char Siu Bao), *13*, 20, *21*
Hsu, Timothy, 76–81, *77*

J

Jewish cooking, Taro Hash Cakes and, 117
Joe's Steamed Rice Rolls, New York, 84

K

Kale Sweet Potato Wontons, *52–53*, 54–55
Kong, Wun Gaw, xiv, 11, 22, 24, 28, 32, 166–67, *167*, 176, 178, 183, 192, 193, 197
Kwong, Joanne, 118–25, *119*

L

lap cheong (Chinese sausage), 6
latkes, Taro Hash Cakes and, 117
Lee's Garden, New York, 32
Lettuce, Shiitake Mushrooms and, *200*, 201
lotus:
  Paste, Fried Sesame Balls with, 223–24, *225*, *234–35*
  Seed Buns, Steamed, 232, *235*
Lum, Mei, 204–11
Lunar New Year, x, 37, 110, 236–40
Lung Fong, New York, 99

M

Maasbach, Nancy Yao, 150–55, *151*
Mandarin's Tea Room, New York, *77*, *78*, *80*, 80–81
Mantao, *12*, 14, *18*, 19
Master Fillings, 7–9, 40–43
  No Pork No Shrimp, 43
  Pork, 41
  Shrimp, 42

Mei Li Wah Bakery, New York, 14
Mid-Autumn Festival, 26, 28, 228
Moon Cakes, 228–30, *229*
    served during Mid-Autumn Festival, 26, 28,
        228
MSG, 4
Museum of Chinese in America (MOCA), New
    York, 125, 150–55, *151, 152, 154*
mushrooms, *see* shiitake mushrooms

N

Nationalist-Communist civil war, 24–26, 150–52
Ng family (Po Wing Hong), 132–37
Nom Wah Nolita, New York, x, xv, 22, 49, 56, 117,
    144
Nom Wah Tea Parlor, New York, *viii, xi, xii,* 99
    dumpling production at, 32–33
    history of, ix–xvi, 24–29
    teas served at, 76–81
noodle(s), 138–49
    Char Siu, *142,* 143
    Garlic Eggplant, *138,* 144, *145*
    Ho Fun, Soup with Chinese Greens, *148,*
        149
    Pan-Fried, in Superior Soy Sauce, *142,*
        143
    Sloppy Joe (aka Spicy Chicken Bolognese
        Served over Wheat Noodles), 146–47
    Tofu, Szechuan, 141
No Pork No Shrimp Master Filling, 43

O

oil:
    chili, 6
    toasted sesame, 3
oyster sauce, 4

P

Pace Act (1875), 206
Pancakes, Scallion, 112–13

pan-fried:
    Chicken and Cabbage Dumplings, 46, *47*
    Noodles in Superior Soy Sauce, *142,* 143
    Pork Dumplings, House Special, *44,* 45
pan-frying, 11
pantry, 3–6
Pearl River Mart, New York, 118–25, *119, 121,*
    122, 155
Peking Duck, *190,* 202, *203*
Phoenix Buns, Steamed, 233, 234–35
pickled red chili, 6
Pickles, Tiger Beer, 215
porcelain, at Wing on Wo, 204–11, *205–8*
pork:
    Bacon and Shrimp Balls, *156–57,* 160
    Belly and Taro Casserole, Cantonese-Style,
        198, *199*
    Char Siu Bao (House Special Roast Pork
        Buns), *13,* 20, *21*
    Char Siu Family Meal, *182,* 183
    Char Siu Noodles, *142,* 143
    in Chinese cooking, 41
    Chops, Salt-and-Pepper, *168, 177,*
        178–79
    Chops, Sweet-and-Sour, 178–79
    Dumplings, Pan-Fried, House Special,
        30–31, 44, 45
    Fried Wu Gok, 73–74, *75*
    Master Filling, 41
    Shanghainese Soup Dumplings (Xiao Long
        Bao), 70–72, *71*
    Siu Mai, *64,* 65
    Steamed Bean Curd Skin Rolls, 93–95,
        94
    Steamed Sparerib Rice Rolls, 92
    Steamed Spareribs, 180, *181*
Potato Chorizo Dumplings with Dill Chimichurri
    Sauce, *53,* 58–59
potato starch, 5
Po Wing Hong, New York, 132–37, *133–36*

R

Red Bean Buns, Steamed, 232
red chili, pickled, 6
rice, 4–5, 126–31
    Egg Fried, 129
    fried, 128–29
    Shrimp and Egg Fried, *128,* 129
    sticky, or glutinous (also called sweet rice),
        4, 131
    Sticky, with Chinese Sausage, *126, 130,* 131
rice flour, 5
rice noodle rolls, Cantonese-style (cheung fun),
    84–92, *85*
    Cilantro and Scallion, *82–83, 86,* 89
    Plain, *82–83,* 87, *162*
    Shrimp, *82–83,* 89
    Sparerib, Steamed, 92
    Sweet Dipping Sauce for, 87
    Vegetable, *82–83, 86,* 92
    Youtiao (Fried Dough), 90, *91*
rice noodles, in Ho Fun Noodle Soup with
    Chinese Greens, *148,* 149
rice wine vinegar, 4
rolls, 82–101
    Egg, OG, 99–100, *101*
    Spring, 96, *97*
    see also Bean Curd Skin Rolls, Steamed; rice
        noodle rolls, Cantonese-style (cheung
        fun)

S

Salt-and-Pepper Pork Chops, *168, 177,* 178–79
Salt-and-Pepper Shrimp, *169, 176, 177*
Sambal Kewpie, 164, 165, *165*
sambal oelek, 6
sauces:
    Chili, 218
    Dill Chimichurri, 58–59
    Dumpling Dipping, 35
    Sweet-and-Sour, 178, 179
    Sweet Dipping, 87
sausage, Chinese (lap cheong), 6
    Sticky Rice with, *126, 130,* 131
    Turnip Cakes, 114–15, *115*
scallion:
    and Cilantro Rice Rolls, *82–83,* 89
    Pancakes, 112–13
September 11, 2001 attacks, xiv, 124, 150, 209–10
Sesame Balls, Fried, with Lotus Paste, 223–24,
    225, 234–35
sesame oil, toasted, 3
Shanghainese Soup Dumplings (Xiao Long Bao),
    70–72, *71*
Shaoxing wine, 4
shiitake mushrooms (black mushrooms):
    dried, 5–6
    Egg Rolls, OG, 99–100, *101*
    and Lettuce, *200,* 201
    No Pork No Shrimp Master Filling, 43
    Turnip Cakes, 114–15, *115*
shrimp:
    and Bacon Balls, *156–57,* 160
    Balls, *156–57,* 160–63, *161*
    Bean Curd Skin Rolls, Steamed, *94,* 95, *162*
    in Chinese cooking, 41
    and Chive Har Gow, *30–31,* 69, *69*
    Crab Claw Balls, Fried, *162,* 163
    dried, 5
    dried, in Sticky Rice with Chinese Sausage,
        126, 130, 131
    and Egg Fried Rice, *127, 128,* 129
    in Fried Wu Gok, 73–74, *75*
    Har Gow, *30–31,* 67, 68–69, *69*
    Master Filling, 42
    in Pork Master Filling, 41
    Rice Rolls, *82–83,* 89
    Salt-and-Pepper, *169, 176, 177*
    Siu Mai, *64,* 65
    and Snow Pea Leaf Har Gow, *30–31,* 69, *69*
    Walnut, 193–94, *195*

Silk Road, xiv–xv, 14, 80

siu mai, 33, 60–65, *61*

    Chicken, 63, *64*

    how to make, 62

    Pork, *64,* 65

    Shrimp, *64,* 65

Sloppy Joe Noodles (aka Spicy Chicken
    Bolognese Served over Wheat Noodles),
    146–47

Snow Pea Leaf and Shrimp Har Gow, *30–31,* 69,
    69

soup(s):

    Dumplings, Shanghainese (Xiao Long Bao),
        70–72, *71*

    Edamame Dumplings in, 51, *51*

    Ho Fun Noodle, with Chinese Greens, *148,*
        149

soy sauce:

    dark, 3

    light, 3

    Superior, Pan-Fried Noodles in, *142,* 143

Sparerib(s), Steamed, 180, *181*

    Rice Rolls, 92

spatulas, or wok chuans, 2

spiders, 2

spoons:

    long-handled mesh (spider), 2

    wok, 2

Spring Rolls, 96, *97*

squid, in Shrimp Master Filling, 42

steamed dessert buns, 231–33

    Lotus Seed, 232, *235*

    Phoenix, 233, 234–35

    Red Bean, 232

Steamed Sparerib(s), 180, *181*

    Rice Rolls, 92

steamers, 2

steaming, 10–11

sticky rice, or glutinous rice (also called sweet
    rice), 4, 131

Sticky Rice with Chinese Sausage, *126, 130,*
    131

stir-frying in a wok, 11

straw mushrooms, in Edamame Dumplings, *48,*
    49–50

Stuffed Eggplant, *174,* 175

Sweet-and-Sour Pork Chops, 178–79

Sweet Dipping Sauce, 87

Sweet Potato Kale Wontons, *52–53,* 54–55

Szechuan Tofu Noodles, 141

T

Tai Pan Bakery, New York, 14

Tang Gum Wor (Uncle Wally Tang), ix, x, xiii,
    xiv, xv, 24–29, *25,* 41, 99, 166, 192, 197, 222,
    227, 228

taro (root):

    Fried Wu Gok, 73–74, *75*

    Hash Cakes, *116,* 117

    and Pork Belly Casserole, Cantonese-Style,
        198, *199*

teas, 76–81

techniques, 10–11

Tiger Beer Pickles, 215

toasted sesame oil, 3

tofu:

    at Fong On, 184–89

    Noodles, Szechuan, 141

    skin (*see* bean curd, dried; Bean Curd Skin
        Rolls, Steamed)

Toishan, Toisanese immigrants, ix, x–xiii, 24, 28,
    56, 58, 186, 206

Tong On Association, New York, 24, 28, 41,
    192

towels, cotton kitchen, 2

Triple C (Chinese Chopped Cheese) Dumplings,
    52, 58–59

Tsao, Sophia Ng, 132–37, *133*

Turnip Cakes, 114–15, *115*

Twin Marquis brand, 33

U

"uncle," as term of respect, 24

V

vegan dishes:
- Cheung Fun, Plain, *82–83*, 87, *162*
- Edamame Dumplings, *48*, 49–50
- Edamame Dumplings in Soup, 51, *51*
- No Pork No Shrimp Master Filling, 43
- Pickles, Tiger Beer, 215
- Scallion Pancakes, 112–13
- Sesame Balls, Fried, with Lotus Paste, 223–24, *225, 234–35*
- Spring Rolls, 96, *97*
- Sweet Potato Kale Wontons, *52–53*, 54–55
- Vegetable Bean Curd Skin Rolls, Steamed, 95
- Vegetable Rice Rolls, *82–83, 86*, 92
- *see also* steamed dessert buns

vegetable:
- Bao, *12*, 22–23
- Bean Curd Skin Rolls, Steamed, 95
- Rice Rolls, *82–83, 86*, 92
- Spring Rolls, 96, *97*

vegetable dishes, 212–19
- Cucumbers, Garlic Chili, 218, *219*
- Greens, Chinese, with Oyster Sauce, *212–13, 216*, 217
- Pickles, Tiger Beer, 215

vermicelli noodles, in Edamame Dumplings, *48*, 49–50

vinegar, rice wine, 4

W

Wally, Uncle, *see* Tang Gum Wor (Uncle Wally Tang)

Walnut Shrimp, 193–94, *195*

wine:
- aji-mirin, 4
- Shaoxing, 4

Wing on Wo, 204–11, *205–8*

wok chuans, 2

wok lids, 2

wok rings, 2

woks, 1–2
- stir-frying in, 11

Wong, Freeman, 102–7, *103*

wontons, 33
- Sweet Potato Kale, *52–53*, 54–55

wood ear mushrooms, in No Pork No Shrimp Master Filling, 43

W.O.W. Project, 204, 211

wrappers:
- fillings vs., 7–9
- preferred brand of, 33
- store-bought vs. homemade, 33

Wu Gok, Fried, 73–74, *75*

Wun Gaw, *see* Kong, Wun Gaw

X

xanthum gum, fortifying vegetarian filling with, 49

xiao long bao, 33

Xiao Long Bao (Shanghainese Soup Dumplings), 70–72, *71*

Y

Yi Ji Shi Mo Noodle Corp, New York, 84

Youtiao (Fried Dough), 90, *91*

yu choy:
- Edamame Dumplings in Soup, 51, *51*
- Ho Fun Noodle Soup with, *148*, 149

Z

Zhuge Liang, 14

ABOUT THE AUTHORS

WILSON TANG has owned and operated the famed Nom Wah Tea Parlor—New York's first dim sum restaurant—since 2010. Since taking over the family business, Tang has grown the restaurant group's footprint to encompass fast-casual and full-service concepts, along with partnerships, in New York, Philadelphia, and Shenzhen, China. His entrepreneurial spirit has been recognized and featured in various national print and cable media, including: *Bon Appétit*, the *New York Times*, NBC *News*, AMC, Food Network, and Travel Channel. Tang lives in the Financial District—a few blocks away from the original restaurant—with his wife, Mae, and his children, Ryan and Lucy.

JOSHUA DAVID STEIN is an author and editor living in Brooklyn. He is the coauthor of *Notes from a Young Black Chef*, *Il Buco Essentials*, *Food and Beer*, and *Epicurean Journeys*, and the author of *To Me, He Was Just Dad*. He served as the U.S. editor for the bestselling *Where Chefs Eat*. Stein is the editor at large at *Fatherly*, a contributing editor at *Food & Wine*, and the former restaurant critic for the *New York Observer* and the *Village Voice*. His work has appeared in *New York*, the *New York Times*, *Esquire*, *GQ*, the *Guardian*, and many other outlets.

ecco

HarperCollins books may be purchased for educational, business, or sales promotional use. For information, please email the Special Markets Department at SPsales@harpercollins.com.

Ecco® and HarperCollins® are trademarks of HarperCollins Publishers.

FIRST EDITION

DESIGNED BY RENATA DE OLIVEIRA

Library of Congress Cataloging-in-Publication Data has been applied for.

ISBN 978-0-06-296599-8

20 21 22 23 24   TC   10 9 8 7 6 5 4 3 2 1